READINGS ON

ALL MY SONS

OTHER TITLES IN THE GREENHAVEN PRESS LITERARY COMPANION SERIES:

AMERICAN AUTHORS

Maya Angelou
Stephen Crane
Emily Dickinson
William Faulkner
F. Scott Fitzgerald
Robert Frost
Nathaniel Hawthorne
Ernest Hemingway
Arthur Miller
Flannery O'Connor
Eugene O'Neill
Edgar Allan Poe
John Steinbeck
Mark Twain
Walt Whitman
Thornton Wilder

AMERICAN LITERATURE

The Adventures of Huckleberry Finn
The Adventures of Tom Sawyer
Black Boy
The Call of the Wild
The Catcher in the Rye
The Crucible
Death of a Salesman
Ethan Frome
Fahrenheit 451
A Farewell to Arms
The Glass Menagerie
The Grapes of Wrath
The Great Gatsby
My Ántonia
Native Son
Of Mice and Men
The Old Man and the Sea
One Flew Over the Cuckoo's Nest
Our Town
The Pearl
A Raisin in the Sun
The Red Pony
The Scarlet Letter
A Separate Peace
The Short Stories of Edgar Allan Poe
To Kill a Mockingbird
Twelve Angry Men

THE GREENHAVEN PRESS
Literary Companion
TO AMERICAN AUTHORS

READINGS ON

ALL MY SONS

Christopher J. Smith, *Book Editor*

Bonnie Szumski, *Series Editor*

Greenhaven Press, Inc., San Diego, CA

Every effort has been made to trace the owners of copy-righted material. The articles in this volume may have been edited for content, length, and/or reading level. The titles have been changed to enhance the editorial purpose. Those interested in locating the original source will find the complete citation on the first page of each article.

Library of Congress Cataloging-in-Publication Data

Readings on All my sons / Christopher J. Smith, book editor.
    p. cm. — (The Greenhaven Press literary companion to American literature)
   Includes bibliographical references and index.
   ISBN 0-7377-0689-9 (lib. bdg. : alk. paper). —
ISBN 0-7377-0688-0 (pbk. : alk. paper)
   1. Miller, Arthur, 1915– All my sons. 2. Domestic drama, American—History and criticism. 3. Fathers and sons in literature. 4. Businessmen in literature. I. Smith, Christopher J., 1963–   II. Series.

PS3525.I5156 A735   2001
812'.52—dc21   200117057
                                              CIP

Cover photo: World Wide Photo/The Bridgeman Art Library
Library of Congress, 26

Copyright © 2001 by Greenhaven Press, Inc.
PO Box 289009
San Diego, CA 92198-9009
Printed in the U.S.A.

"During an idle chat in my living room, a pious lady from the Middle West told of a family in her neighborhood which had been destroyed when the daughter turned the father into the authorities on discovering that he had been selling faulty machinery to the Army. . . . By the time she had finished the tale I had transformed the daughter into a son and the climax of the second act [of All My Sons] *was full and clear in my mind."*

—Arthur Miller, Introduction to
The Collected Plays

CONTENTS

Chapter 1: Two Perspectives from the Author

1. Storming the Fortress of Unrelatedness
by Arthur Miller   46

Ten years after the Broadway debut of *All My Sons*, Arthur
Miller wrote a detailed outline of the play's origins and
how it marked a vital step in his development as a playwright.

2. Remembering *All My Sons* by *Arthur Miller*   53

Arthur Miller remembers the tensions surrounding the
first production of *All My Sons*, its critical reception in
1947, and the way subsequent productions broadened his
own understanding of his first successful play.

Chapter 2: Themes

1. World War II and the Burden of Moral Responsibility in *All My Sons* by *Sheila Huftel*   60

Through the medium of the tragic sacrifices of those who
were killed in World War II, *All My Sons* explores the
themes of moral commitment and the need to confront
hard truths.

2. The Public and Private Environments of *All My Sons* by *Tom Scanlan*   67

Through the Keller family, Arthur Miller dramatizes the
costs of retreating into family life at the expense of the
larger social environment.

3. The Challenge of Being Moral in a Corrupt World
by Benjamin Nelson   74

A great deal of corruption occurs in the name of family
loyalty in *All My Sons;* finding a judgment in favor of an
individual's moral obligation to society is the thematic task
the play sets for itself.

FOREWORD

*"'Tis the good reader that
makes the good book."*

Ralph Waldo Emerson

The story's bare facts are simple: The captain, an old and scarred seafarer, walks with a peg leg made of whale ivory. He relentlessly drives his crew to hunt the world's oceans for the great white whale that crippled him. After a long search, the ship encounters the whale and a fierce battle ensues. Finally the captain drives his harpoon into the whale, but the harpoon line catches the captain about the neck and drags him to his death.

A simple story, a straightforward plot—yet, since the 1851 publication of Herman Melville's *Moby-Dick*, readers and critics have found many meanings in the struggle between Captain Ahab and the whale. To some, the novel is a cautionary tale that depicts how Ahab's obsession with revenge leads to his insanity and death. Others believe that the whale represents the unknowable secrets of the universe and that Ahab is a tragic hero who dares to challenge fate by attempting to discover this knowledge. Perhaps Melville intended Ahab as a criticism of Americans' tendency to become involved in well-intentioned but irrational causes. Or did Melville model Ahab after himself, letting his fictional character express his anger at what he perceived as a cruel and distant god?

Although literary critics disagree over the meaning of *Moby-Dick*, readers do not need to choose one particular interpretation in order to gain an understanding of Melville's novel. Instead, by examining various analyses, they can gain numerous insights into the issues that lie under the surface of the basic plot. Studying the writings of literary critics can also aid readers in making their own assessments of *Moby-Dick* and other literary works and in developing analytical thinking skills.

The Greenhaven Literary Companion Series was created with these goals in mind. Designed for young adults, this unique anthology series provides an engaging and comprehensive introduction to literary analysis and criticism. The essays included in the Literary Companion Series are chosen for their accessibility to a young adult audience and are expertly edited in consideration of both the reading and comprehension levels of this audience. In addition, each essay is introduced by a concise summation that presents the contributing writer's main themes and insights. Every anthology in the Literary Companion Series contains a varied selection of critical essays that cover a wide time span and express diverse views. Wherever possible, primary sources are represented through excerpts from authors' notebooks, letters, and journals and through contemporary criticism.

Each title in the Literary Companion Series pays careful consideration to the historical context of the particular author or literary work. In-depth biographies and detailed chronologies reveal important aspects of authors' lives and emphasize the historical events and social milieu that influenced their writings. To facilitate further research, every anthology includes primary and secondary source bibliographies of articles and/or books selected for their suitability for young adults. These engaging features make the Greenhaven Literary Companion Series ideal for introducing students to literary analysis in the classroom or as a library resource for young adults researching the world's great authors and literature.

Exceptional in its focus on young adults, the Greenhaven Literary Companion Series strives to present literary criticism in a compelling and accessible format. Every title in the series is intended to spark readers' interest in leading American and world authors, to help them broaden their understanding of literature, and to encourage them to formulate their own analyses of the literary works that they read. It is the editors' hope that young adult readers will find these anthologies to be true companions in their study of literature.

INTRODUCTION

Released to critical acclaim and commercial success in 1947, *All My Sons* was Arthur Miller's breakthrough play. It established him as a new and important voice in American drama. Nevertheless, like many of Miller's plays, *All My Sons* has been somewhat overshadowed by the monumental success of *Death of a Salesman* (1949), the play that followed. Often, the only thing theatergoers and lovers of drama know about *All My Sons* is that, like *Death of a Salesman*, the play involves a deep and far-reaching conflict between a father and his son, and this conflict has important moral implications for what Miller sees as deeper problems within American society as a whole. Although it is true that there are thematic connections between the two plays, this view tends to diminish the undeniable power of *All My Sons*—and the fact that it should be judged as an outstanding achievement in and of itself.

All My Sons represented a watershed moment in the development of morally committed, realist drama in America. Arthur Miller came of age in the 1930s and '40s, when the entire world was convulsed by a devastating economic depression and the most destructive war humankind has ever experienced. In the wake of these traumatic decades, Miller's work was shaped by the belief that writers and artists have a responsibility to explore and expose the contradictions and injustices inherent in their society. *All My Sons* communicates an urgent need for an all-embracing commitment to humankind, yet it manages to do so without preaching to its audience. Through the medium of fundamentally recognizable, decent human beings, Miller subtly explores the conflict between an individual's love for his family and his duty to others. Joe Keller is a kind and loving man, yet in the course of doing what he thought was best for his family, he committed an unforgivable crime. The implications of this crime grow with each act of *All My Sons*, leading to an explosive confrontation that exposes the true cost of pursuing the American dream. The play's conclusion unnerved audiences over fifty years ago, and it is a testament to the enduring power of *All My Sons* that it still asks a great deal of audiences today.

Readings on All My Sons presents a collection of the best criticism written on this play during the last fifty years. From the earliest critical responses to Miller's own recollections of the play forty years after he wrote it, this volume illustrates the richness and enduring appeal of a vital contribution to twentieth-century American drama.

Arthur Miller: A Biography

Just as Arthur Miller's plays offer penetrating glimpses into American life in the twentieth century, his long and productive life seems to have moved in step with many of the crucial events that shaped the "American" century. Success and public adulation came to Miller relatively early in his career with *Death of a Salesman* (1949), but he never allowed this success to compromise his ongoing efforts to probe American society for its deeper truths; and it hasn't stopped him from asking unsettling questions about what he sees as America's narrow and unquestioning belief in the truth and goodness of the American dream. From the depths of despair that characterized the 1930s depression in America, to the shameful persecutions of McCarthyism in the 1950s, to the struggle for worldwide human rights, readers and historians will many years from now turn to Arthur Miller's life and literary output to understand the complexities and ironies of twentieth-century life.

Growing Up in 1920s New York

Arthur Miller was born in New York City on October 17, 1915, the second child of Isodore and Augusta Miller. Arthur was the grandchild of Jewish immigrants—his grandparents on both sides had grown up in Poland and emigrated in the 1880s—and he grew up in comfortable circumstances amid a passionate and eccentric family. The Millers lived in a large and quite exclusive uptown apartment. Arthur's memories of his youth included summers spent at Far Rockaway Beach, adventures in Central Park with his brother Kermit, and unforgettable trips to movies, vaudeville shows, and the theater. Miller later acknowledged that, as a youth, he preferred the theater because the human presence of actors on the stage rather than the screen was such an overwhelmingly "real" experience for him.

As an indication of the radically different time and culture in which Miller grew up, one need only look at how a centuries-old Jewish tradition determined the course of his mother's life. According to Miller, "She was . . . haunted by a world she could not reach out to, by books she would not get to read, concerts she would not get to attend, and above all, interesting people she'd never get to meet."[1] An exceedingly intelligent woman, she was nevertheless "traded into an arranged marriage within months of graduating *cum laude* from high school."[2] As the only one in the family who had a deep interest in literature, drama, and music, Augusta Miller was an important influence on her son, and Miller remembers the two of them sharing a special emotional bond in his early years.

Miller's father, Isodore, was a marked contrast to his wife. Left behind in Poland until his parents could afford his passage to America, he crossed the Atlantic at the age of seven unaccompanied by any friends or family. Isodore Miller grew up in a two-room apartment in New York City with his parents and five brothers and sisters, and their tiny apartment was also used as a sewing room for the emerging family business. Obliged from a very early age to work as his parents struggled to establish themselves in America, Isodore only received a few months' schooling and never learned to read or write. Despite his illiteracy, by 1920 he had managed to build one of the three largest coat factories in the country at that time. Arthur Miller's relationship with his father was complicated.

In many ways, the Miller family was a testimony to the American dream: The grandparents had come to America with nothing, but they laid the groundwork for their children to succeed in a way that would have been impossible in their native country. Amid the optimism of the 1920s, it appeared that a bright and limitless future was spread out before Arthur's generation. The depression would destroy this sense of an inevitable, generational progression up the social ladder, but in his autobiography *Timebends: A Life,* Miller acknowledges his deep and abiding debt to his cultural background:

> This desire to move on, to metamorphose—or perhaps it is a talent for being contemporary—was given me as life's inevitable and rightful condition. To keep becoming, always to stay involved in transition. It was all [my mother] and my father had ever known. She was born on Broome Street on the Lower East Side of Manhattan, her father, Louis Barnett, a clothing contractor, one of the struggling mass down there.

. . . Like Samuel, my father's father, Louis came from the Polish hamlet of Radomizl, and they were probably distantly related, I have always thought, because they resembled one another. . . . They had all been transforming themselves since they were children in Europe, even before the emigration of the 1880s seemed possible, living as they did in a cultural twilight zone between the Austrian-German language and influence, the Polish peasantry, and their Jewish identity.[3]

Unlike other major Jewish American writers of the twentieth century, such as Philip Roth, Joseph Heller, and Saul Bellow, Miller's Jewish origins are not placed at the forefront of his writing; however, in his autobiography he makes it clear that his upbringing shaped many of his plays. Besides Jewish characters in his plays *Incident at Vichy* (1964) and *The Price* (1968), Miller remembers that while writing about the Puritans in *The Crucible* (1953), "I felt strangely at home with these New Englanders, moved in the darkest part of my mind by some instinct that they were putative ur-Hebrews, with the same fierce idealism, devotion to God, tendency to legal reductiveness, the same longings for the pure and intellectually elegant argument."[4] In the wake of the Holocaust, Miller also acknowledges that if his grandparents hadn't decided to leave Poland for the United States, he probably would not have lived to see the age of thirty.

THE DEPRESSION

The 1929 stock market crash plunged the Miller family into a degree of poverty and desperation that they would have thought unthinkable only a year before. Their financial strains became apparent in 1929: Not only was their chauffeur let go and their car sold, but they could no longer afford the mortgage on their Manhattan home and moved to Brooklyn to economize. The family would be forced to move once more to an even smaller, cheaper house, and Arthur Miller remembered the ever-present fear that the family would lose this home and end up on the streets. Arthur's older brother, Kermit, had to drop out of college to help his father with the coat business, which was rapidly heading toward bankruptcy. And while he was still at Abraham Lincoln High School, Arthur's day began at four in the morning, when he would deliver bread around the neighborhood for a local bakery in order to supplement the family income.

Since he had compensated for his lack of education by securing wealth and success as a businessman, Isodore Miller was shattered by the failure of his business—and his family's precarious financial future. Miller remembers how his father became more and more powerless, and later he reflected on how, with the onset of the depression, "A fine dusting of guilt fell upon the shoulders of the failed fathers, and for some unknown number of them there would never be a recovery of dignity and self-assurance, only an endless death-in-life down to the end."[5] Correspondingly, failed father figures who stake everything on success in the business world—only to experience deep and abiding failure—feature largely in Miller's plays. Meanwhile, his mother, Augusta, became increasingly contemptuous of her husband's inability to restore their former wealth. When the need for money grew desperate, she had to gradually sell off all her jewelry, often had to charm the bank manager into putting off mortgage payments on the house, and at times turned her mastery of bridge into high-stakes games for money.

In 1933, Arthur Miller graduated from high school. Though he had briefly entertained the idea of making his living as a singer, he saw his graduation as something of a disaster, since he was now just another unemployed young man among millions. However, he was fortunate to eventually find a job at an auto parts warehouse—Chadick-Delamater—which paid the then princely sum of fifteen dollars a week. In his 1955 one-act play *A Memory of Two Mondays*, Miller would remember the anti-Semitism he encountered from the mostly Irish American workers at Chadick-Delamater, the grinding monotony of the work itself, and the employees' constant fears of being fired at a time when there was no other work anywhere. The job lasted until the summer of 1934, when Miller left to enroll at the University of Michigan; his savings from the job helped pay for his tuition.

FOUR YEARS AT THE UNIVERSITY OF MICHIGAN

The road to admission into the University of Michigan had not been an easy one for Arthur Miller. During high school, he had flunked algebra three times and had been expelled from several classes; not surprisingly, his teachers had refused to write him the necessary letters of recommendation. Miller was turned down twice before he finally managed to convince the University of Michigan that he was ready to become a serious student.

In 1934, the University of Michigan was regarded as one of the most politically radical campuses in America, and Miller's intellectual curiosity and growing interest in Marxism matched well with this highly charged atmosphere. Like many young men of his generation, Miller had witnessed firsthand the devastating effects of the depression and the government's indifference to the suffering of so many people. By the early 1930s, it seemed to Miller that capitalism had failed and that two stark choices faced the world: fascism or communism. Horrified by the threat that Adolf Hitler posed to the world, Miller saw Marxism as offering the best answer to America's economic stasis and growing sense of despair about the future. In fact, some of Miller's classmates volunteered to fight in the Spanish Civil War against the fascist Francisco Franco, whom Hitler was supporting, and many of them paid for their political convictions with their lives.

Miller's life at Michigan was frenetic yet personally enriching. Not only was he holding down two part-time jobs while enrolled in a full academic schedule, but he also worked for the school's highly political newspaper, the *Michigan Daily*. Most important, though, was Miller's decision to seriously begin writing plays. He took courses with Professor Kenneth Rowe, whom he would later acknowledge as a formative influence on his work. At the same time, Miller was reading and becoming deeply influenced by the psychological complexity and confrontation with social issues present in the works of nineteenth-century Russian writers Leo Tolstoy, Fyodor Dostoyevsky, and Anton Chekhov, and the Scandinavian dramatists Henrik Ibsen and August Strindberg. The depression also influenced the purpose of Miller's writing, as he believed in exposing social injustice and communicating the urgent need for morally grounded political action.

In these circumstances Miller's apprenticeship as a writer began. Because of his precarious financial situation, Miller set his sights on winning one of the Avery Hopwood Awards, which awarded cash prizes ranging from $250 to $1,250—extraordinarily large sums for that time—for plays written by undergraduates. In 1936 and 1937, he realized his ambitions, winning Hopwood Awards for his plays *No Villain* (1936) and *Honors at Dawn* (1937). His 1937 play *They Too Arise* failed to win a Hopwood Award, but captured the Theater Guild Award, which paid $1,250. All three plays anticipated his later successes *All My Sons* (1947) and *Death of a Salesman* (1949), using the family as a medium to explore ideas of political commitment and conflicting social values. However, these early plays were far less subtle than his mature masterpieces. They reflected the propagandistic kind of drama being produced in America in the 1930s, when playwrights felt an obligation to have their characters bombastically state their undying allegiance to a worthy political cause.

MILLER'S STRUGGLES IN THE EARLY 1940S

Miller's four years at Michigan were rewarding and important, since he was able to develop his deepest social and political views and freely create drama with the encouragement of his professors. In June 1938, he received his bachelor of arts degree and then traveled to New York to work for the New York Federal Theater Project—a government-funded organization that helped directors and actors keep theater alive in America at a time when nobody could really afford to attend plays. Miller's tenure with the Federal Theater Project was short-lived however, since Congress withdrew funding in 1939. After being on unemployment for a few months, Miller turned to writing radio plays, for which he earned $100 a script. His radio plays alternated between light entertainment and attempts to advocate left-wing political causes. Miller derived little satisfaction from writing them, but America was still in economic straits and money was hard to come by.

In 1940, Miller married Mary Grace Slattery, whom he had met at the University of Michigan, and for the next four years the couple struggled to make a living in New York. Mary worked as both a waitress and an editor at Harper and Brothers, while Miller now wrote patriotic plays for both the radio and stage to aid the war effort. He also assisted a shipfitter in the Brooklyn Navy Yard once America had become directly involved in World War II. Miller's interest in Marxism intensified throughout the war years, as the threat that fascism posed to world freedom grew more and more evident and alarming.

A high school football injury in 1932 had seriously damaged Miller's knee ligaments and kept him out of active military service. As the war went on, Miller anguished over some meaningful way to contribute to the war effort. This same sense of responsibility would later find a voice in *All My Sons'* Chris Keller. In 1944, Miller visited army camps around

America, gathering material for a screenplay, *The Story of G.I. Joe*. The film was based on war correspondent Ernie Pyle's sketches of military life in Europe, which were collected and published under the title *Here Is Your War*. Although Miller withdrew from the project as it became clear that his control of the script was going to be compromised—the first of his many frustrations in dealing with Hollywood—his sympathy and admiration for combat soldiers fighting the fascist threat was apparent in the work that emerged from his interviews, *Situation Normal* (1944).

Miller's first Broadway play, *The Man Who Had All the Luck*, also appeared in 1944, but it was something of a disaster, lasting only four performances and deeply discouraging him in his resolve to remain a professional playwright. *The Man Who Had All the Luck* focuses on David Frieber, who has through a succession of chance occurrences managed to establish himself as a prosperous businessman. A model of the self-made man, Frieber thinks he is something of a fraud and that he doesn't deserve his success. The play sets in motion a series of questions concerning American culture's flawed notion of what constitutes success—an important preoccupation in Miller's writing.

To pay off the financial losses from *The Man Who Had All the Luck*, Miller published the first of the only two novels he has ever written, *Focus* (1945). The novel is about anti-Semitism and its destructive psychological effects on both Jews and Gentiles. The novel's main character, an anti-Semite named Lawrence, is repeatedly mistaken for a Jew after he begins to wear glasses. Therefore he is for the first time exposed to the violent realities of being a Jew in a hostile, anti-Semitic world. Slowly, his views begin to change, and at the end of the novel, he refuses to correct a police officer who assumes he is Jewish. Emerging as it did at the end of World War II, just as the true horror of Hitler's Holocaust was coming to light, *Focus* was particularly relevant and illustrated Miller's ability to tap into the most significant moral questions of his time—a gift that would continue over the next three decades.

THE SUCCESS OF *ALL MY SONS*

In 1945, though, Miller was consumed by a sense of inadequacy: He felt that, at thirty years of age, his early successes as a playwright at the University of Michigan were now distant memories in light of his more recent failures. Miller remembers his resolve to make *All My Sons* his last shot at fame on Broadway: "I would hold back this play until I was as sure as I could be that every page was integral to the whole and would work; then, if my judgment of it proved wrong, I would leave the theater behind and write in other forms."[6] Miller would spend nearly two years writing this play, until he was certain it represented his absolute best.

All My Sons had its origins in an actual incident: Miller's mother-in-law in Ohio told him the story of a young girl who had turned her father in to the FBI for knowingly manufacturing and selling faulty aircraft parts during the war. The conflict embedded in this incident—between acting on one's moral convictions and upholding one's loyalty to family—developed into the thematic focus of Miller's new play. Miller adjusted the story somewhat to express this theme through the conflict between a father and his son, but the idea of exposing greed and betrayal as the foundation of a family's prosperity remained. Set in the immediate aftermath of the Second World War, *All My Sons*' appeal to audiences and emotional impact were immediate and lasting. The production, directed by Elia Kazan, opened in January 1947 and ran for 347 performances; it also won the coveted New York Drama Critics' Circle Award and was later developed into a successful film. Miller had been handed his first dose of public success, and it disconcerted him to such an extent that for a brief period of time he took a job in a box factory so that he wouldn't lose his grip on reality. However, he now had the leisure to travel and write without financial pressures.

DEATH OF A SALESMAN

Throughout much of 1947 and 1948, Miller was drawn to the docks of Brooklyn. He sensed a compelling story in the rampant political corruption and network of organized crime that controlled this multi-million-dollar conduit for goods in and out of America. Miller befriended union organizers and came to know the largely Italian American community that made its precarious living from working on the docks. Without knowing it, he was conducting research into a later play, *A View from the Bridge.* Miller's venture into this largely unknown part of New York City led to his traveling to Europe with a union organizer, Vincent Longhi, where he saw how much World War II had devastated European culture and intellectual life.

Miller's imagination was also consumed at this time by a character that had lodged in his mind years ago when he was growing up in Brooklyn. Miller had grown up in a family of salesmen, and the nature of their job had always fascinated him. In his uncle and aunt, Manny and Annie Newman, and their two sons Buddy and Abby, Miller divined what would become the archetypal Loman family. According to Miller, Manny Newman's fiercely competitive streak, his absurd illusions of success, and "the river of his sadness" that flowed beneath all he did made a deep and lasting impression.

Sensing this character's significance, Miller patiently waited for Willy Loman to spring to life fully formed in his imagination. In 1948, the success of *All My Sons* allowed him to buy a small farm in Connecticut. Miller had been an enthusiastic carpenter since his teenage years, and he immediately set about building a small cabin where he could write undisturbed, meditating on the play he intended to write there. Once the cabin was completed, he wrote *Death of a Salesman* in six weeks, although he remembers writing the first act in one especially intense twenty-four-hour session. After he completed the manuscript, Miller sent the play to Elia Kazan, who had directed *All My Sons*, and then nervously awaited Kazan's response. Like millions after him, Kazan was deeply moved by *Death of a Salesman*. He agreed to direct it, and the play opened on Broadway in January 1949.

Death of a Salesman represented an enormous artistic advance for Miller, since he abandoned the strict realism of *All My Sons* in favor of a looser and more fluid form that charted the interior life and ultimate destruction of salesman Willy Loman. In keeping with Willy's precarious state of mind, the present action is constantly invaded by brief yet revealing incidents from the past, until past and present seem to merge into one continuous, uninterrupted flow. *Death of a Salesman* is many things: a psychological portrait of individual disintegration, a chilling indictment of the American dream, and a painful yet epic confrontation between a father and his son. However one chooses to interpret the play, there is no doubt that, in Willy Loman, Arthur Miller created a character that has become a permanent part of the American imagination. Reviewers and audiences were unanimous in their praise of the play, and *Death of a Salesman* established Arthur Miller as America's most important living playwright. The play won the New York Drama Critics' Circle Award and the Pulitzer Prize, and ran for a remarkable 742 performances.

ARTHUR MILLER AND THE COLD WAR

Although Arthur Miller was now extremely wealthy and internationally famous, he had to confront the burden that every writer who meets with enormous success and acclaim has to bear—he would now be forever known and defined by one work. Indeed, despite writing many other excellent plays, Miller has never been able to match the success of *Death of a Salesman*, which he wrote when he was only thirty-four. The 1950s would be a time of both personal and public turmoil for Miller. He felt oppressed by the growing political hysteria over the Communist threat in America, and it would have an enormous effect on his life and career. However, he continued to write well, and at least one of the plays he wrote in the 1950s is considered by many to be the equal of *Death of a Salesman*.

The year 1949 marked a dramatic shift in the balance of political power in the world—a shift that induced widespread panic in the United States. That year, the Soviet Union successfully tested an atom bomb, and there was a Communist revolution in China. Suddenly, the United States saw itself as losing the fight for world domination, as the Soviet military could no longer be cowed by America's former monopoly on atomic weaponry and communism had gained a vital strategic foothold in Asia. A wave of fear and suspicion gripped the nation, and Senator Joseph McCarthy spearheaded the internal political response by initiating what came to be known as the "witch hunts" for former Communist sympathizers in America. Like many men and women in the 1930s and early 1940s, Arthur Miller had embraced Marxism, since it seemed the only humane alternative to the breakdown of free market capitalism in America and the rise of fascism in Germany, Italy, and Spain. With the end of World War II, the cherished illusions about communism and the Soviet Union shared by Miller and many of his contemporaries were destroyed as evidence of outrageous human rights abuses slowly became known. Soviet leader Joseph Stalin was revealed as nothing more than another totalitarian ruler who had sent millions to their deaths in his rise to power in the 1930s, and who now suppressed intellectual and political freedom in both the Soviet Union and Eastern Europe.

With these revelations, any illusions about the Soviet Union disappeared. Yet Senator McCarthy now used the House Un-American Activities Committee (HUAC) to subpoena, expose, and humiliate former Communist sympathizers at all levels of American society. Nobody was ever convicted, since they hadn't committed a crime. However, the important thing for the committee was to have individuals who were brought before it publicly confess the error of their ways and expose other former Communist sympathizers. In order to save his career, Elia Kazan, who had directed *All My Sons* and *Death of a Salesman,* named nine people in the motion picture industry whom he knew were former members of the Communist Party. To Miller, this insidious process of persecution was an outrage, since the committee threatened the bonds of trust between individuals by coercing people into betraying others.

Many of Miller's friends who worked in film and theater—writers, actors, directors, and producers—were ostracized and couldn't find employment. Essentially their careers were destroyed, since everyone feared reprisals if they were seen associating with people who were out of favor with the all-powerful committee. Because of the success of his plays and the financial security they had earned for him, Miller was not as vulnerable; however, throughout the early 1950s, he noted with alarm the oppressive conformity of American society, and the complete intolerance extended to anyone who questioned McCarthyism. Miller's first work after *Death of a Salesman* was his adaptation of Norwegian playwright Henrik Ibsen's *An Enemy of the People* in 1950. A powerful portrayal of the destruction of a principled individual's standing in society at the hands of an irrational mob, *An Enemy of the People* was a thinly disguised indictment of the spirit of early 1950s America. Yet as if to illustrate the power that rigid social and political conformity exerted over all aspects of America at this time, the play failed and the production soon closed down.

THE CRUCIBLE: MILLER'S RESPONSE TO POLITICAL OPPRESSION

The response to McCarthyism for which Miller will be forever remembered, though, came in the form of his 1953 play, *The Crucible.* As the HUAC hearings developed and the lives and careers of more and more individuals were destroyed, Miller became convinced that, like the 1692 Salem witch trials, the

HUAC hearings represented "evidence of an imploded community that distrust and paranoia had killed."[7] What struck Miller once he began researching the hysteria that gripped Salem was how, like the HUAC hearings, what was demanded above all was an almost ritualistic public confession of guilt and that nothing less than a full confession would allow an individual to reenter society. The play's main character, John Proctor, refuses to confess to spurious charges of witchcraft, even though a confession will save his life. As a result he is hanged, but Proctor's resolve to remain truthful to himself and others, even at the cost of his life, upholds the power of the individual in society. In the conformist climate of the early 1950s, when the state seemed to be dictating how people should think and feel, Miller believed that "an individual conscience was all that could keep a world from falling."[8] A potentially explosive play, *The Crucible* was, according to Miller, "cooled off" by a rather austere production, and it did not have a long run on Broadway. Miller remembers how professional acquaintances of many years refused to speak with him on opening night, and the play put him firmly in the sights of HUAC, further marking him as a left-wing dissenter.

Two years later, though, *The Crucible* reopened in a small, independent New York theater, and it played successfully for two years. Reflecting on the fact that the play continues to be produced all over the world, Miller believes *The Crucible* moved beyond its association with McCarthyism a long time ago. In its advocacy of a morally grounded individual conscience triumphing over mob hysteria and state oppression, Miller believes *The Crucible* will continue to speak to any community or society besieged by "either a warning of tyranny on the way or a reminder of tyranny just past."[9] As if to confirm Miller's judgment of the play, the reverence critics and audiences alike have for *The Crucible* has never diminished, and many now see it as the equal of *Death of a Salesman*.

MILLER'S APPEARANCE BEFORE HUAC

Between 1953 and 1956, it was obvious to Miller that he was out of favor with both the government and the entertainment industry, and they intended to make him aware of their displeasure. While *The Crucible* had made his view of McCarthyism plain, his much-publicized criticism of director Elia Kazan's decision to cooperate with HUAC had earned him the hostility of conservative forces in the entertainment industry. In 1953, his application for a new passport, so he could travel to Belgium to see the European premiere of *The Crucible*, was denied. A State Department representative informed Miller that his traveling to Europe at this time was "not in the national interest." In 1955, Miller accepted an offer to write a script for a television film on gang violence among New York City's youths. After spending a great deal of time with the city's youth workers and writing a detailed outline, politics suddenly intervened. In a series of events typical of the McCarthy era, Miller was publicly attacked in the *New York World-Telegram* for his leftist political leanings, and the paper demanded that he be removed from the project. As a result of the article, federal and local authorities voted that his participation in the New York City Youth Board film end. In a manner that chillingly reflected *The Crucible*, one board member objected to the fact that Miller would not "repent" for his former Communist sympathies.

The attacks continued, and Miller was finally subpoenaed to appear before HUAC in June 1956. At the hearing, Miller defended his former activities in left-wing and Communist-sponsored organizations, and made plain his opposition to the committee's immense power, its harassment of individuals, and indeed its very existence in a democracy. Most important, Miller refused to name any writers he knew who had attended Communist Party meetings. Miller's refusal to cooperate with the committee was consistent with his belief in the need to act according to the dictates of one's own conscience, no matter what the cost. However, in doing so he had broken the law, and he was convicted for contempt of Congress in May 1957. Miller now faced imprisonment, but throughout 1957 and 1958, public support for his position grew, and the conviction was finally overturned. Miller's victory over HUAC coincided with a general public reaction against the excesses of McCarthyism, which had destroyed the lives and careers of many people who posed no threat to national security whatsoever. Miller would continue to take public and at times controversial stances regarding individual rights throughout the 1960s and '70s, but by 1958 his fight with McCarthyism was over.

ARTHUR MILLER AND MARILYN MONROE

Miller had written two one-act plays in 1955, *A View from the Bridge* and *A Memory of Two Mondays*. The first play drew on his investigation into the Italian American community that worked at the Brooklyn shipyards; the second recalled his experience working in the auto parts warehouse Chadick-Delamater during the depression. Compared with *The Crucible*, these were minor works, and the response from both critics and audiences was disappointing. However, one year later Miller would develop *A View from the Bridge* into a powerful full-length play. A passionate, unsettling dramatization of betrayal and incestuous desires, *A View from the Bridge* has a strange yet enduring position among Miller's dramatic works. Its stature continues to grow, and like *Death of a Salesman* and *The Crucible*, it has undergone many successful revivals.

From 1956 to 1961, in addition to his conflict with HUAC, Miller experienced changes in his private life: He divorced his first wife, Mary Grace Slattery, and subsequently married Marilyn Monroe. Miller had first met Monroe in 1950 when he had visited Hollywood with Elia Kazan to pitch a film about union corruption on the New York waterfront. They did not renew their friendship until 1954; by that time, Monroe had divorced baseball star Joe DiMaggio and Miller's marriage was rapidly disintegrating. Miller does not discuss the breakup with Mary in his autobiography *Timebends: A Life*, so the source of their discord is unknown. What is known is that he was increasingly seen socially with Monroe throughout 1955, and they were married in June 1956 after he obtained a divorce.

Marilyn Monroe and Arthur Miller were followed by the media throughout their marriage.

Miller and Monroe were married for four and a half chaotic and tumultuous years, during which time Miller tried—and ultimately failed—to infuse her life with some degree of stability. Not even the fame Miller secured with *Death of a Salesman* could possibly have prepared him for the barrage of media attention Marilyn Monroe constantly drew.

Miller was angered yet resigned to the media's destructive determination to portray Monroe as nothing more than a sex symbol, while ignoring her ambitions of becoming a serious actress.

When Monroe became pregnant and miscarried late in 1957, Miller sought to allay her depression by developing a short story of his, "The Misfits," into a screenplay in which she would have a starring role. The film was eventually directed by John Huston, and Monroe starred alongside Clark Gable and Montgomery Clift. However, the filming itself, which took place in 1958, was plagued by delays as Monroe became increasingly depressed and addicted to painkillers and sleeping pills. By the time *The Misfits* was completed, Miller and Monroe's marriage had been irrevocably damaged. They lived apart for most of 1960 and divorced in January 1961. Just over a year and a half later, Monroe died from an overdose of sleeping pills. Embittered by the publicity and media sensationalism that had destroyed her life and now surrounded her death, Miller did not attend the funeral and refused all interviews.

MILLER IN THE 1960s

A year after his divorce from Marilyn Monroe, Miller married Inge Morath, an Austrian photographer he had met on the set of *The Misfits.* He slowly returned to serious writing, which— with the exception of the screenplay for *The Misfits*—he had all but abandoned from 1956 to 1961. After a slow start, Miller wrote two plays in rapid succession: *After the Fall* (1964) and *Incident at Vichy* (1964). Through its main character Quentin, *After the Fall* explores innocence and guilt at both the individual and collective levels, and it quite explicitly draws on people and events from Miller's life. For this reason, reviewers savaged the play. They accused Miller of shamelessly and self-indulgently exploiting his past relationships—especially with Marilyn Monroe—in order to therapeutically exorcise his personal demons. However, the play is consistent with Miller's meditations on the place of individual responsibility and morality in a post-Holocaust, nuclear age, and on the enigma of humans' almost limitless capacity to inflict suffering on one another. Despite the negative reviews, and because of the notoriety that soon surrounded the play, people flocked to see *After the Fall.* Miller quickly wrote *Incident at Vichy*, a play that emerged from his observations of trials of former Nazis held in Frankfurt, Germany, in March 1964. Miller's direct examination of the murder of Jews by the Nazis during World War II was roundly castigated—this time for sacrificing dramatic action in favor of extended sermonizing on the need for individual responsibility.

Though Miller's plays were increasingly criticized and ignored in America, they were widely praised and appreciated in Europe—a trend that has continued to this day. Ever since the two-act version of *A View from the Bridge* successfully debuted in London in 1956, Miller had often traveled to Europe to consult with directors producing his plays. In the course of his travels he met many European writers, and in 1965 he was asked to take on the presidency of PEN, an international organization of poets, editors, essayists, and novelists. Miller accepted, and he used his position to advocate artistic freedom around the world and to fight for the release of writers imprisoned in Eastern European and third world countries. Miller would remain the president of PEN until 1972. In that time he traveled widely and successfully transformed the organization into a powerful pressure group that worked to establish basic human rights for writers around the world. In keeping with his commitment to human rights, Miller refused to allow his work to be published in Greece in 1969 as a protest against the Greek government's oppression of writers; in the following year, the Soviet Union banned his books because of his criticism of their human rights record and his support of Soviet dissident writers such as Aleksandr Solzhenitsyn.

Not surprisingly, Miller was also active on the home front. By 1967, America was engaged in a heated and often violent debate over the war in Vietnam and the ever-enlarging presence of American combat troops in that country. Miller was vocal in his support of the antiwar movement, publishing a widely read article in the *New York Times* that condemned American involvement in Vietnam and pointed out the cruel irony and hypocrisy of American soldiers forcibly removing Vietnamese peasants from their land and burning their villages in order to "protect" them from the Communist Vietcong. In 1968, Miller was part of the Connecticut delegation at the Democratic National Convention in Chicago, where he unsuccessfully tried to force a vote on a resolution in favor of ending the bombing of North Vietnam, and the commencement of talks to end the war altogether.

Despite Miller's wide and active involvement in the tumultuous political and social upheavals of the late 1960s, he did manage to write another full-length play, *The Price*, which opened on Broadway in 1968. *The Price* marked something of a departure for Miller. Though it was characteristically autobiographical, it was an apolitical family drama that introduced a comic dimension that hadn't been as readily apparent in Miller's previous work. Essentially a family drama examining the resentments and recriminations that exist between two brothers—one who has sacrificed a great deal for his family and another who has subsequently been freed by this sacrifice to pursue his dreams—*The Price* draws on Miller's relationship with his brother Kermit and the emotions surrounding the death of their mother and father in the 1960s. Despite the mixed reviews, *The Price* was Miller's most successful play since *Death of a Salesman*, running for 425 performances in New York before moving on to London in March 1969.

A CONTINUING COMMITMENT TO DRAMA AND HUMAN RIGHTS

Miller would publish three plays from 1970 to 1980—*The Creation of the World and Other Business* (1972); *The Archbishop's Ceiling* (1976); and *The American Clock* (1980)—none of which were successful when they were first produced. However, both *The American Clock* and *The Archbishop's Ceiling* were later enormously successful in England. Indeed, since the revised two-act version of *A View from the Bridge* opened in London rather than on Broadway, Miller has consistently found a more sympathetic and appreciative audience in England; the reception of his plays in America, on the other hand, has continued to be ambivalent. Miller attributes this trend to the increasingly commercial nature of Broadway, which he has dubbed the "Frightened Theater" because of its tendency to immediately close a play down if it appears that it is not going to become a financial hit for its investors. In order to assure some degree of financial success, producers tend to opt for safe, artistically unadventurous plays that will draw as many people as possible. Miller also notes that, unlike on Broadway, where the *New York Times* can either make or break a play, no single critic or newspaper in England is powerful enough to destroy a production with one negative review.

Now in his eighties, Miller continues to be prolific. *Danger: Memory!* (1987) and *Broken Glass* (1994) are particularly impressive plays, and in the last twenty years he has published a great deal of nonfiction, including his outstanding autobiography, *Timebends: A Life.* The 1980s and '90s, however, were mostly characterized by revivals of his greatest successes from the 1940s and '50s. In 1983 he visited China to direct *Death of a Salesman*; one year later, *Death of a Salesman* resurfaced on Broadway with Dustin Hoffman starring as Willy Loman in a much-publicized and successful Broadway production that was later turned into an equally successful television production; long-running, well-received productions of *The Crucible* and *The Price* followed; and in 1996 *The Crucible* was turned into a powerful film starring Daniel Day Lewis and Winona Ryder.

Miller has always been remarkably consistent in following the dictates of his conscience, no matter what the personal cost, and in asserting the obligation of individuals to act against social and political injustices. He continued to speak out against political regimes in the Soviet Union, Czechoslovakia, Brazil, Iran, and Nigeria that forcibly suppressed and imprisoned writers for political views that diverged from the party line. He constantly pressured both the United Nations and the American government to adopt uncompromising stands on the issue of human rights, maintaining that any country or institution that said nothing in the face of such outrages against humanity was in danger of becoming a "moral nullity." Miller's activism was local as well as national and international in its scope. From 1973 to 1978, in his home state of Connecticut, Miller worked tirelessly to secure the release of Peter Reilly, a young man police coerced into confessing to the murder of his mother, even though an enormous amount of evidence supported Reilly's innocence. This almost instinctive appetite for addressing injustice at all levels of society has been a hallmark of Miller's adult life.

In the 1980s, Miller received many public honors and became something of an unofficial ambassador for American literature and international human rights. In 1984, he was awarded the prestigious Kennedy Center Lifetime Achievement Award. The irony that the award banquet was held in the same room in which he had faced the House Un-American Activities Committee nearly thirty years earlier was not lost on Miller. In 1986, nearly fifteen years after his work had been banned in the Soviet Union, he met Mikhail Gorbachev, who claimed that he had read all of Miller's plays and admired them deeply. These events signaled the extent to which this remarkable man's equally remarkable contribution to twentieth-century life and literature had finally been recognized.

It is too early to assess Miller's ultimate impact on American literature. While *Death of a Salesman* and *The Crucible* already have an undisputed place among America's greatest literary achievements, the fate of Miller's other work is much more open to debate. There is, however, no question about the consistency and humanity of Miller's writing, moral convictions, and commitment to activism. They have remained in tune with each other throughout his adult life and together form a remarkably coherent whole. Whatever the final critical judgments of Miller, ongoing revivals of his work illustrate their continuing power to unsettle and move audiences throughout the world.

NOTES

1. Arthur Miller, *Timbends: A Life.* New York: Grove, 1987, p. 17.
2. Miller, *Timebends*, p. 18.
3. Miller, *Timebends*, p. 5.
4. Miller, *Timebends*, p. 42.
5. Miller, *Timebends*, p. 113.
6. Miller, *Timebends*, p. 244.
7. Miller, *Timebends*, p. 339.
8. Miller, *Timebends*, p. 342.
9. Miller, *Timebends*, p. 348.

CHARACTERS AND PLOT

CHARACTERS

Doctor Jim Bayliss: A neighbor of the Kellers and a good friend of Chris Keller. Bayliss is a successful doctor, but as Miller's description of him acknowledges, there is a "wisp of sadness about him." The reason for this sadness is that he feels he is something of a fraud treating wealthy patients who never really have anything seriously wrong with them. At the end of the play he describes how happy he was as a young man in New Orleans, when he was poor but doing important medical research. He admits, though, that there was no money to be made in his research. Under pressure from his wife, he has set up a successful, but for him meaningless, practice in Ohio. In his friend, the war hero Chris Keller, he sees a man who has fixed, noble principles, and this makes Bayliss feel a sense of inadequacy that he sacrificed the medical research that was so important to him for the sake of financial security.

Sue Bayliss: Dr. Jim Bayliss's wife. A former nurse who helped finance her husband's medical school education, she is a down-to-earth woman who always speaks her mind. Money is important to her, and Sue Bayliss realizes how supporting Jim in school meant that she could ultimately force her husband to compromise his ideal of doing medical research in favor of a lucrative medical practice. She is also aware that Jim resents her for it, and for this reason, she in turn resents Chris Keller, because as she puts it, Chris "makes people want to be better than it's possible to be." In a vengeful yet truthful act, Sue tells Ann that she thinks Chris is a hypocrite, since everyone in the neighborhood knows Joe Keller got away with murder, and deep down Chris knows he did too.

Bert: The Bayliss's eight-year-old son. Bert appears twice in the play and talks with Joe Keller, who has a somewhat revealing running joke with Bert that there is a jail in the Kellers' basement.

Ann Deever: The former neighbor and fiancée of Larry Keller, a World War II pilot who has been missing for more than three years and is presumed dead. Ann now lives in New York, but she has returned to her hometown in Ohio at the request of Larry's brother Chris, who loves her and wants to marry her. She is an attractive, sensitive, and vulnerable young woman who has been damaged by both the death of her former boyfriend and the fact that her father was convicted of knowingly selling defective parts to the military, which cost the lives of twenty-one pilots. Yet Ann is also strong and resolute in deciding what she wants from her life. Unlike Kate Keller, she has moved on from Larry's death, and she is determined to overcome the objections of her brother, George, and Chris's mother, Kate, and marry Chris. In the play's final act, Ann illustrates the lengths to which she will go to secure what she wants by showing Kate Keller the despairing, suicidal letter Larry wrote her the day he went missing. Though the revelation of the letter has tragic consequences, it is instrumental in freeing Ann and Chris to marry, cast off the past, and build a new life independent of the sins of their fathers.

George Deever: Ann's brother, a lawyer in New York. George returns to the Keller household to confront Joe Keller and accuse him of being involved in the crime that sent his father, Steve Deever, to prison. Now that he has finally heard his father's side of the story, George is full of remorse that he and Ann chose to turn their backs on him. George now wants to wrest a confession of guilt from Joe Keller and put a stop to Ann and Chris's impending marriage. Although he is rightly angry and embittered over the destruction of his family, he is also compassionate; this is illustrated by his warm response to Kate Keller and Lydia Lubey, whom he always liked. George is unsuccessful in turning Ann against Chris Keller, but his visit sets in motion the chain of events that finally lead to Joe Keller's admission of guilt.

Steve Deever: The father of both Ann and George, and the former business partner and neighbor of Joe Keller. Presented as a weak, indecisive man, Steve Deever is in prison after being convicted of knowingly selling defective engine parts to the military during World War II. Although Steve Deever does not actually appear in the play, his presence is important, since so much of the action depends on the mystery that surrounds Joe Keller's involvement in the scandal that sent Deever to prison. Through Joe Keller, Steve Deever is also connected to the death of Larry Keller, and the scandal surrounding his criminal act also hangs over the proposed marriage of Chris Keller and his daughter, Ann.

Chris Keller: The eldest son of Joe and Kate Keller, and brother of Larry Keller. Chris is described in the play as "a man capable of immense affection and loyalty," and as someone who "makes people want to be better than it's possible to be." These qualities arise from his war experiences; he feels a sense of guilt for the men who died under his command, and a corresponding sense of responsibility to make those men's sacrifice mean something. Somewhat haunted by the fact that his father made a fortune from the war, he nevertheless works for his father and enjoys the benefits of his father's wealth. As a war veteran, Chris despises Steve Deever for indirectly killing twenty-one American pilots because of his greed; however, he ignores his deepest, unspoken suspicions that perhaps his own father was involved. When Joe Keller is finally exposed, Chris sees the last of his ideals die, and true to the belief that there is an obligation to others greater than the obligation to one's family, he is prepared to turn his father in to the authorities. Chris Keller's conflicts and his final resolution embody the overarching theme of *All My Sons:* In the final analysis, "there's a universe of people outside and you're responsible to it."

Joe Keller: The father of Chris and Larry Keller, and the husband of Kate Keller. Joe is around sixty years of age, deeply practical, and a businessman to the core. The question of whether or not Joe Keller sold defective parts to the military so that his business might survive is the central question of *All My Sons.* Joe Keller's strongest character traits are his unconditional love for and sense of loyalty to his family, and his readiness to do anything in his power to preserve his family's financial security. Passing the highly successful family business he has built on to his son Chris is clearly his fondest hope. Ironically, though, this sense of loyalty led to his committing a criminal act, which in turn is responsible for his son Larry's suicide. Unlike his son Chris, Joe cannot see a larger world beyond that of his family, and therefore he does not feel the moral responsibility toward others that his son Chris does. Even when his involvement in his company's crime is exposed, Joe still feels that he hasn't done anything wrong, since he did it to save his business and therefore his family's wealth. It is only when he reads his son Larry's suicide note that he finally admits he should have seen all the men fighting in the war as his sons. The extent to which he finally takes responsibility and feels despair for the loss of life his actions brought on is indicated at the play's end when he commits suicide.

Kate Keller: The mother of Chris and Larry Keller, and the wife of Joe Keller. Kate Keller's grief over her son Larry's death in the war is so intense that she has only a tenuous hold on her sanity. The only way she can contain her grief is by believing that he has been "missing" for three years and that someday he will return. Kate is also somewhat cruel and manipulative. In order to maintain her illusion that Larry is alive, she will not under any circumstances accept Ann and Chris's love for each other; she wants Ann to remain single and lonely, as a kind of monument to Larry. Yet as the play develops, a deeper reason emerges for her wanting to believe that Larry is still alive. Crushed by her secret knowledge of Joe Keller's involvement in selling defective parts to the military, her only way of ignoring the fact that her husband is a murderer is to obsessively believe that somewhere her son is still alive. Even after Joe Keller admits his guilt to his son, Kate is certain that she can convince Chris to let the family business continue as it is and that in a way Joe's admission of guilt is positive because Ann will no longer want to marry Chris. Yet when Ann produces Larry's suicide note, Kate is crushed, and her final desire is to free her living son, Chris, from the burden of his father's sins.

Larry Keller: Brother of Chris Keller and the youngest son of Kate and Joe Keller. Like Steve Deever, Larry Keller is never physically present during the play, but nevertheless he is a constant presence throughout. The only direct assessment of his character comes from Joe Keller, who, after his confession of guilt and subsequent rejection by Chris, proclaims that Larry's loyalties always lay with his family and the family business. Yet when Larry finally speaks for himself through the suicide note he wrote to Ann, we see that Larry's loyalties, like those of Chris, lay with his fellow soldiers.

Frank Lubey: A neighbor of the Kellers and the husband of Lydia Lubey. Frank is something of a well-meaning, good-natured fool who has the tendency to appear on the scene at inopportune moments and embarrass people by saying the wrong thing. An ardent believer in astrology, he is also constructing Larry's horoscope for Kate Keller, and therefore he assists in maintaining her illusory belief that her son is alive. Frank is a successful man who, unlike Chris Keller and George Deever, wasn't drafted during the war and therefore avoided all the horrors they experienced.

Lydia Lubey: A neighbor of the Kellers and the wife of Frank Lubey. Lydia is an attractive, vivacious young woman, and everyone likes her. She appears only briefly in the play, but George Deever is particularly pleased to see her, and her presence offsets some of the anger he feels toward the Kellers.

PLOT SUMMARY

All My Sons is set in the years immediately following the end of World War II, in the backyard of a family home in a prosperous suburb somewhere in Ohio. The action begins early on a Sunday morning, with the family patriarch Joe Keller and his neighbor Doctor Jim Bayliss reading the newspaper together. Strangely and quite ominously, they share the stage with the ruined stump and branches of a young apple tree that has been blown over the night before. Another neighbor, Frank Lubey, joins them almost immediately, and for a while their conversation is light and desultory. However, when Frank notices the ruined apple tree, the conversation turns more serious, and we find out that the tree was planted as a memorial to the Kellers' son Larry, who fought in the war and has been missing for almost three years now. Frank's admission that, at the request of Kate Keller, Joe's wife, he is making a horoscope for Larry adds a degree of tension to the dialogue, since we are made to wonder why Kate Keller wants Frank to construct a horoscope for her son who, in spite of the fact that his body has not been found, is almost certainly dead.

Frank and Jim's wives soon appear to call their husbands home, and Joe Keller talks briefly with Sue Bayliss and Lydia Lubey. Again the conversation is light, but there is a tense undertone to it, as we find out that Larry's girlfriend Ann Deever, who used to live next door in what is now the Bayliss house, has come to visit the Kellers. The dialogue again arouses questions in the minds of the audience, such as why the girlfriend of a man who has been missing and presumed dead for three years is visiting and why her parents don't live next door anymore.

Sue and Lydia soon exit and we are then introduced to Chris Keller—the elder Keller son who fought in and returned from the war. They discuss the broken tree, and Joe suggests that they tell Kate about it before she comes out and has to see it for herself. Chris replies that his mother was out in the garden at four in the morning when it broke. According to Chris, who woke to the sound of the tree cracking, at the moment the tree blew over his mother ran into the kitchen and cried the rest of the night, which causes Joe to reflect that, three years later, she is still acting "just like after he died." For both Chris and his father there is no question in their minds that Larry is dead, yet it is obvious that Kate still cherishes the hope that he is alive and will one day miraculously return. Chris believes that they need to confront his mother with the facts, but his father maintains that as long as "there's no body and no grave" she will refuse to be convinced that her son is dead.

Chris then tells his father he has something important to discuss with him, something that will take the tension already surrounding Larry Keller's absence to a more intense level. Chris invited Ann Deever to visit because he is in love with her, and he intends to ask her to marry him. His father doesn't appear to be particularly surprised, but he doesn't appear particularly happy about it either, and he brings up the obvious problem: "From mother's point of view [Larry] is not dead. . . . You marry that girl and you're pronouncing him dead." The conversation also reveals that Joe Keller has a successful business that he desperately wants to pass on to his son. Chris knows this and gives his father something of an ultimatum: If he is forced to choose between marrying Ann and preserving his mother's hopes that Larry is still alive, he will marry Ann, move away with her, and start over somewhere else.

At this moment, Kate Keller appears, and she quickly directs the conversation toward Larry and her belief that Ann has come back because she too believes he is alive and will someday return. To Chris this is deluded, evasive talk, and he bluntly tells his mother, "we ought to put our minds to forgetting him . . . we never took up our lives again. We're like at a railroad station waiting for a train that never comes in." Kate ignores the substance of what he is saying and asks

Chris to get her an aspirin; while he is away we find out
what a strong-willed yet obsessive woman Kate Keller is.
She senses that Chris has invited Ann so that he can ask her
to marry him, and as far as she is concerned this must not
happen. Kate angrily and firmly tells her husband, "I want
you to act like [Larry's] coming back. Both of you. . . . Because if he's not coming back, then I'll kill myself!" Kate im-
pulsively sees the destruction of the memorial tree the same
night Ann returned as a sign that Larry is going to return,
and she ends the conversation by telling Joe Keller, "You
above all have got to believe," to which Joe defensively responds, "What does that mean, me above all?" Clearly there
is a terrible secret buried in the heart of the Keller family.

The argument ceases with the reappearance of Chris, and
this time Ann is with him. Beneath the banter that follows
there is an unsettling tension, which breaks out into the
open when Ann discovers that Kate has kept all Larry's
clothes and shined all his shoes as if he is going to return
any day. This revelation deeply disturbs Ann, and she immediately senses that Kate is seeking out another ally to bol-
ster her belief that Larry is still alive. Ann bluntly puts an
end to any such thoughts, stating that she is not waiting for
Larry, and she is incredulous that Kate is clinging to the
hope that Larry is ever coming home. Kate persists in trying
to convince Ann, though, and the tension is again briefly
broken with the entrance of another character—the reappearance of Frank Lubey.

Frank is delighted to see Ann, but when he asks about
Ann's father, the major conflict of the play—which all the
action has been moving toward—is revealed. We learn that
Joe Keller and Ann's father, Steve Deever, were business
partners during the war, and they were both jailed for manufacturing defective cylinder heads for airplane engines.
These defects directly led to the deaths of twenty-one pilots.
Joe Keller was exonerated and went on to build a successful
business, but Ann's father was found guilty of attempting to
cover up the flaws in the defective parts and then selling
them to the military. As a result, he is now in prison. Neither
Ann nor Chris can forgive Steve Deever, but strangely Joe
Keller feels compassion for him, which both confuses and ir-
ritates his son.

When Joe goes inside to make a dinner reservation for
later that night, Chris Keller is finally left alone with Ann

and given the chance to declare his love for her and ask if she will marry him. Ann acknowledges that the reason she never married after Larry was declared missing was that Chris started writing to her and she was waiting for him to make his intentions clear. With Ann reciprocating his love, Chris feels that an enormous burden has been lifted from his shoulders and that together they can move on with their lives and find happiness. When Ann asks why he took so long to share his feelings for her, Chris talks movingly about how for a long time his war experiences made him feel guilty about having survived while others died, and feel ashamed about the source of his father's wealth. What the war taught Chris was an abiding sense of solidarity, a sense of "the love a man can have for a man" and that "you've got to be a little better because of that." The picture of Chris Keller that emerges from this dialogue is a man determined to act with a deep moral sense so that the sacrifices of those who died in the war will mean something. However, his ambivalence toward his father's wealth, and the fact that he is the one who will inherit money that has "blood on it" makes him profoundly uneasy.

Suddenly Joe Keller returns and announces that Ann's brother, George, is on the phone and wants to speak to her. George's phone call has made Joe anxious, and again the question arises as to why Joe should feel anxiety about the Deever family when he has been declared innocent of any involvement in Steve Deever's crimes. In connection with this unease, he announces to his son that he wants to name his company "Christopher Keller, Incorporated," and that Chris should not feel ashamed, because the money the company has earned is "good money, there's nothing wrong with that money." As Chris and his father talk, the audience is able to hear Ann speaking with her brother on the telephone, and her sense of unease concerning what George is saying becomes more and more apparent. The first act ends with Ann's announcement that her brother is coming to visit, and Kate Keller's strange fear that George Deever is going to bring with him accusations and revelations that will shatter the Keller family.

Act 2 begins late in the afternoon of the same day, with Chris sawing off the top of the broken tree from its stump and throwing it away. Kate Keller comes out into the yard and shares with Chris her fears that Steve Deever—who al-

ways maintained that Joe Keller was involved in the attempted cover-up of the defective parts—has shared evidence with his son that will lead to the case being reopened.
Nevertheless, her panic does not diminish her attempts to
manipulate her son. Kate maintains that, since the trial, the
Deever family, including Ann, has hated the Kellers, and
Chris should tell George when he arrives to take Ann back
to New York with him. When Ann comes into the yard again,
Kate immediately goes back inside, and Chris soon follows
to get dressed for dinner.

Adding to the tension Ann feels regarding her brother's
arrival, the Kellers' neighbor Sue Bayliss comes into the
yard, searching for her husband; however, he has gone to
pick George Deever up from the train station. A somewhat
abrasive conversation develops between the two in which
Sue says she is sick of living next door to the "Holy Family"
and that "Everybody knows Joe pulled a fast one to get out
of jail." Ann is shaken and angry, and when Chris returns
she confronts him about his father, making it plain that if
Joe Keller is guilty and Chris knows it then she couldn't possibly marry him. Chris maintains that his father is innocent
and that he has always believed in his father's innocence,
and when Joe Keller reenters the scene the couple are once
again reconciled. In anticipation of George's arrival, Joe
mentions that he would be happy to use his influence to find
a position for a bright and promising lawyer such as George
Deever and that he wouldn't hesitate to find work for Ann's
father once he gets out of jail. Ann is shocked and Chris is
once again mystified and angry that Joe seems to have forgiven his former partner. When Joe goes back inside to see
if his wife is ready to go out to dinner, George Deever finally
appears, and the buried conflict over Joe Keller's guilt or innocence is about to come out into the open.

George arrives feeling angry and confrontational, telling
Chris that Joe Keller destroyed their family, and telling Ann
that it would be an outrage for her to marry Chris. He has
come from visiting his father in jail and is full of remorse
that he and Ann completely turned their backs on him for so
many years. George has also heard Steve's side of the story,
and he is convinced that Joe Keller told his father over the
phone to try to cover up the defects in the cylinder heads by
welding over the cracks. According to George, Joe then
stayed away from the plant, saying he had the flu, and there-

fore Steve could never prove that Joe ordered him to initiate the cover-up. George accuses Chris of lying to himself in believing otherwise, and he tells Ann that everything the Kellers have "is covered with blood." George also brings up the interesting point that, although Chris is the heir apparent to the Keller fortune, he has never had his name put on the business. Chris is momentarily nonplussed by this observation—the implication being that deep down he is ashamed of having his name beside that of his father.

The argument is briefly defused by the appearance of Kate Keller, and then their neighbor Lydia Lubey, since George has always liked them both. Seeing both women causes him to reflect on how much both his family and the Kellers have lost due to the war, but when Joe Keller finally comes out to face his former partner's son, George's anger returns. Joe Keller is obviously prepared for George, and he manages to defend himself well, giving many examples of the mistakes Steve Deever made in his life, how he never accepted the blame for any of those mistakes, and how he always tried to pass the blame on to others.

George is momentarily disarmed by Keller's calm, logical manner, but when Kate proudly claims that her husband not only looks well since George last visited but hasn't been sick for a single day in fifteen years, Keller has to quickly "remind" her of the time he had the flu. Kate's hesitant agreement confirms George's deepest suspicions, but at this tense moment, Frank Lubey comes bursting in, triumphantly holding up Larry's completed horoscope and maintaining that the day Larry became missing was "a favorable day" for him, meaning the odds against anything bad happening to him that day are overwhelming. This rekindles all Kate Keller's hopes regarding Larry's return, further removing her from any possible acceptance of Chris and Ann's engagement. George seizes on Kate's reaction to tell Ann that Kate Keller is effectively telling her to leave, and he asks Ann to go back to New York with him. Kate encourages Ann, saying that she has in fact packed her bag for her, which in turn causes Chris to explode at his mother. As Ann tells George that she intends to stay with Chris, and then follows him down the driveway trying to ease his anger, Chris finally tells his mother that he and Ann are going to marry. For Kate Keller, this is too much, and finally the connection between her deluded belief that Larry is alive and her knowledge of her husband's guilt is made plain in one climactic moment, when she exclaims, "Your brother's alive darling, because if he's dead, your father killed him. Do you understand me now? As long as you live, that boy is alive. God does not let a son be killed by his father. Now you see, don't you? Now you see."

This revelation leads to a decisive confrontation between Joe Keller and his son. Chris finally realizes something he has subconsciously suspected all along: His father is as responsible for the death of twenty-one young pilots as Steve Deever is. It is now obvious why Keller felt so uncomfortable with Ann and Chris's contempt for Steve Deever—by despising Steve for what he did they were effectively passing judgment on Keller himself.

To Chris, his father is now nothing less than a murderer, but Joe Keller tries to justify his actions, maintaining that he would have gone out of business if his company had acknowledged the mistake in their production process, and he tried to cover up the defects for Chris—to save the company he had built for his son. Chris responds by saying that he didn't risk his life at war and watch men he loved die for the sake of the family business, and he asks what kind of man "kills his own." The act ends with Chris leaving the scene weeping, while his father, suspecting he has lost his son forever, calls after him.

The third and final act begins at two o'clock the next morning. Kate Keller is sitting alone in the yard, waiting for her son to return. After a few moments Jim Bayliss comes out to talk with her, and he acknowledges that he has somehow always known Joe Keller was guilty. Kate responds that she thought that Chris must have also suspected his father and that she didn't think it would be quite the shock it was when he finally found out the truth. Jim, who has always respected Chris, responds that to live with the knowledge of what his father did "takes a certain talent . . . for lying" and that while most people have this "talent," Chris doesn't. Jim believes that Chris has gone off to let the last of his ideals quietly die, and to decide what to do with the rest of his life. He then leaves to see if he can find Chris and bring him home.

Joe Keller then comes out, and he still cannot fully understand why Chris has turned on him so decisively, since he lied in order to protect his family and their financial future. Kate responds by saying that, for Chris, "There's something bigger than the family," to which Joe Keller ominously responds, "if there's something bigger than that I'll put a bullet in my head!" Kate says to Joe that the only way to win Chris back would be to say to his son that he would be willing to publicly admit his guilt and go to prison. Joe cannot see how this would help, and in another ominous moment, he claims that Larry was different from Chris, since he was always unquestioningly loyal to the family and its business.

At this point Ann enters, and she immediately calms the Kellers by saying that, even with Joe Keller's admission of guilt, she will not seek to reopen the investigation into the defective parts. However, in return for her silence she demands that Kate acknowledge to Chris that she truly believes Larry is dead, thereby freeing her son to marry Ann without any lingering guilt. Kate refuses, since her heart is set on Ann forever sharing her grief over Larry's loss. Feeling she now has no choice, Ann asks to be left alone with Kate, and then produces a letter that Larry wrote to her just before he disappeared. In the letter, Larry wrote that he has heard about his father and Steve Deever's arrest and the charges against them. He says that he is so ashamed he "can't bear to live anymore," that as soon as he finishes this letter he is going out on a mission, and "They'll probably report me missing."

It is effectively a suicide note, and its impact on Kate is shattering; however, the situation grows worse. Chris returns, full of self-loathing and determined to leave forever because, as he puts it, "I was made yellow in this house because I suspected my father and I did nothing about it." Chris is equally certain that Ann could no longer possibly want to marry him, and he is surprised she hasn't left already. Hearing Chris return, Joe Keller comes down and confronts his son, asking him what he wants to do—whether he wants to give away all the family's money or turn him in. Chris has no real answer for him, because as he says, he knows his father "is no worse than most men but I thought you were better. I never saw you as a man. I saw you as a father. I can't look at you this way, I can't look at myself!"

Feeling that Chris is slipping away from her, Ann snatches the letter from Kate's hands and gives it to him to read. Kate pleads with her son not to read the letter to his father, but out of anger and disgust he does. The letter's effect on Joe Keller is decisive. Determined that he now be held accountable, he asks Chris to get the car so that he can go and turn himself in to the district attorney. He says to his wife that Larry was his son, but Larry believed his father should have seen all the men fighting in the war as his sons and that he should not have endangered their lives because he wished to preserve his own family's economic security. He then goes into the house, supposedly to get his jacket. Chris is determined that his father should go to jail, maintaining that there is a greater world beyond the confines of family and that all individuals need to feel a sense of responsibility toward the well-being of others. Yet as he finishes speaking, a shot is heard inside the house. Stricken with remorse, Joe Keller has killed himself, and the play ends with Chris Keller in his mother's arms. In the final lines Kate is telling her son that he must forget and live, as if she too has been freed in some way by her husband's death.

CHAPTER 1

Two Perspectives from the Author

READINGS ON
ALL MY SONS

Storming the Fortress
of Unrelatedness

Arthur Miller

Ten years after the first performance of *All My Sons*,
Arthur Miller discussed the origins of the play, what
he aimed to achieve by writing it, and his assessment of its strengths and weaknesses. During the
war, Miller heard a story about an Ohio woman who
had turned her father in to the authorities after she
learned that he had been selling faulty machine
parts to the army. From this story, Miller created Joe
Keller's slow awakening to the evil he has done, and
the destruction of his son Chris Keller's illusions.
While acknowledging Norwegian playwright Henrik
Ibsen's profound influence on *All My* Sons, Miller
argues that the play was designed to illustrate "the
full loathesomeness of an anti-social action."

During an idle chat in my living room, a pious lady from the
Middle West told of a family in her neighborhood which had
been destroyed when the daughter turned the father in to the
authorities on discovering that he had been selling faulty
machinery to the Army. The war was then in full blast. By
the time she had finished the tale I had transformed the
daughter into a son and the climax of the second act was full
and clear in my mind.

I knew my informant's neighborhood, I knew its middleclass ordinariness, and I knew how rarely the great issues
penetrate such environments. But the fact that a girl had not
only wanted to, but had actually moved against an erring father transformed into fact and common reality what in my
previous play [*The Man Who Had All the Luck*] I had only
begun to hint at. I had no awareness of the slightest connection between the two plays. All I knew was that somehow a
hard thing had entered into me, a crux toward which it

seemed possible to move in strong and straight lines. Something was crystal clear to me for the first time since I had begun to write plays, and it was the crisis of the second act, the revelation of the full loathesomeness of an anti-social action.

THE QUEST FOR REALISM

With this sense of dealing with an existing objective fact, I began to feel a difference in my role as a writer. It occurred to me that I must write this play so that even the actual criminal, on reading it, would have to say that it was true and sensible and as real as his life. It began to seem to me that what I had written until then, as well as almost all the plays I had ever seen, had been written for a theatrical performance, when they should have been written as a kind of testimony whose relevance far surpassed theatrics.

For these reasons the play begins in an atmosphere of undisturbed normality. Its first act was later called slow, but it was designed to be slow. It was made so that even boredom might threaten, so that when the first intimation of the crime is dropped a genuine horror might begin to move into the heart of the audience, a horror born of the contrast between the placidity of the civilization on view and the threat to it that a rage of conscience could create.

THE QUESTION OF RELATEDNESS

It took some two years to fashion this play, chiefly, I think now, because of a difficulty not unconnected with a similar one in the previous play. It was the question of relatedness. The crime in *All My Sons* is not one that is about to be committed but one that has long since been committed. There is no question of its consequences' being ameliorated by anything Chris Keller or his father can do; the damage has been done irreparably. The stakes remaining are purely the conscience of Joe Keller and its awakening to the evil he has done, and the conscience of his son in the face of what he has discovered about his father. One could say that the problem was to make a fact of morality, but it is more precise, I think, to say that the structure of the play is designed to bring a man into the direct path of the consequences he has wrought. In one sense, it was the same problem of writing about David Beeves in the earlier play, for he too could not relate himself to what he had done. In both plays the dramatic obsession, so to speak, was with the twofold nature of the individual—his own concept of his deeds, and what turns out to be the "real" description of them. *All My Sons* has often been called a moral play, and it is that, but the concept of morality is not quite as purely ethical as it has been made to appear, nor is it so in the plays that follow. That the deed of Joe Keller at issue in *All My Sons* is his having been the cause of the death of pilots in war obscures the other kind of morality in which the play is primarily interested. Morality is probably a faulty word to use in the connection, but what I was after was the wonder in the fact that consequences of actions are as real as the actions themselves, yet we rarely take them into consideration as we perform actions, and we cannot hope to do so fully when we must always act with only partial knowledge of consequences. Joe Keller's trouble, in a word, is not that he cannot tell right from wrong but that his cast of mind cannot admit that he, personally, has any viable connection with his world, his universe, or his society. He is not a partner in society, but an

ALL MY SONS AND HENRIK IBSEN'S RETROSPECTIVE METHOD

In All My Sons, *Arthur Miller adopted Norwegian dramatist Henrik Ibsen's technique of thematically forcing the past into the present—a perfect means of slowly exposing the nature and implications of Joe Keller's crime.*

All My Sons has been described as an Ibsenite play, and certainly, if we restrict Ibsen to the kind of play he wrote between *The League of Youth* (1869) and *Rosmersholm* (1886), it is a relevant description. The similarities are indeed so striking that we could call *All My Sons* pastiche if the force of its conception were not so evident. At the center of the play is the kind of situation which was Ibsen's development of the device of the "fatal secret." Joe Keller, a small manufacturer, has (in a similar way to Consul Bernick in [Ibsen's] *Pillars of Society)* committed a social crime for which he has escaped responsibility. He acquiesced in the sending of defective parts to the American Air Force in wartime, and yet allowed another man to take the consequences and imprisonment. The action begins after the war, and is basically on the lines of what has been called Ibsen's retrospective method (it was always much more than a device of exposition; it is a thematic forcing of past into present). The Ibsen method of showing first an ordinary domestic scene, into which, by gradual infiltration, the crime and the guilt enter and incorporated member, so to speak, and you cannot sue personally the officers of a corporation. I hasten to make clear here that I am not merely speaking of a literal corporation but the concept of a man's becoming a function of production or distribution to the point where his personality becomes divorced from the actions it propels.

The fortress which *All My Sons* lays siege to is the fortress of unrelatedness. It is an assertion not so much of a morality in terms of right and wrong, but of a moral world's being such because men cannot walk away from certain of their deeds. In this sense Joe Keller is a threat to society and in this sense the play is a social play. Its "socialness" does not reside in its having dealt with the crime of selling defective materials to a nation at war—the same crime could easily be the basis of a thriller which would have no place in social dramaturgy. It is that the crime is seen as having roots in a certain relationship of the individual to society, and to a certain indoctrination he embodies, which, if dominant, can

build up to the critical eruption, is exactly followed. The process of this destructive infiltration is carefully worked out in terms of the needs of the other characters—Keller's wife and surviving son, the girl the son is to marry, the neighbours, the son of the convict—so that the demonstration of social consequence, and therefore of Keller's guilt, is not in terms of any abstract principle, but in terms of personal needs and relationships, which compose a reality that directly enforces the truth. If Keller's son had not wanted to marry the convicted man's daughter (and they had been childhood friends; it was that neighbourhood which Keller's act disrupted); if his wife, partly in reaction to her knowledge of his guilt, had not maintained the superstition that their son killed in the war was still alive; if the action had been between strangers or business acquaintances, rather than between neighbours and neighbouring families, the truth would never have come out. Thus we see a true social reality, which includes both social relationships and absolute personal needs, enforcing a social fact—that of responsibility and consequence. This is still the method of Ibsen in the period named, and the device of climax—a concealed letter from Keller's dead son, who had known of his father's guilt—is again directly in Ibsen's terms.

Excerpted from Raymond Williams, "The Realism of Arthur Miller," *Critical Quarterly* 1 (Summer 1959), pp. 140–49.

mean a jungle existence for all of us no matter how high our buildings soar. And it is in this sense that loneliness is socially meaningful in these plays.

To [address] Henrik Ibsen's[1] influence upon this play, I should have to split the question in order to make sense of it. First, there was the real impact of his work upon me at the time: this consisted mainly in what I then saw as his ability to forge a play upon a factual bedrock. A situation in his plays is never stated but revealed in terms of hard actions, irrevocable deeds; and sentiment is never confused with the action it conceals. Having for so long written in terms of what people felt rather than what they did, I turned to his works at the time with a sense of homecoming. As I have said, I wanted then to write so that people of common sense would mistake my play for life itself and not be required to lend it some poetic license before it could be believed. I wanted to make the moral world as real and evident as the immoral one so splendidly is.

But my own belief is that the shadow of Ibsen was seen on this play for another reason, and it is that *All My Sons* begins very late in its story. Thus, as in Ibsen's best-known work, a great amount of time is taken up with bringing the past into the present. In passing, I ought to add that this view of action is presently antipathetic to our commonly held feeling about the drama. More than any other quality of realism, or, to be more exact, of Ibsenism as a technique, this creates a sense of artificiality which we now tend to reject, for in other respects realism is still our reigning style. But it is no longer acceptable that characters should sit about discussing events of a year ago, or ten years ago, when in "life" they would be busy with the present. In truth, the effort to eliminate antecedent material has threatened to eliminate the past entirely from any plays. We are impatient to get on with it—so much so that anyone making a study of some highly creditable plays of the moment would be hard put to imagine what their characters were like a month before their actions and stories begin. *All My Sons* takes its time with the past, not in deference to Ibsen's method as I saw it then, but because its theme is the question of actions and consequences, and a way had to be found to throw a long line into the past in order to make that kind of connection viable.

1. Norwegian playwright Henrik Ibsen (1828–1906) was the most influential dramatist of the nineteenth century.

MILLER'S REVISIONS

That the idea of connection was central to me is indicated again in the kind of revision the play underwent. In its earlier versions the mother, Kate Keller, was in a dominating position; more precisely, her astrological beliefs were given great prominence. (The play's original title was *The Sign of the Archer.*) And this, because I sought in every sphere to give body and life to connection. But as the play progressed the conflict between Joe and his son Chris pressed astrology to the wall until its mysticism gave way to psychology. There was also the impulse to regard the mystical with suspicion, since it had, in the past, given me only turgid works that could never develop a true climax based upon revealed psychological truths. In short, where in previous plays I might well have been satisfied to create only an astrologically obsessed woman, the obsession now had to be opened up to reveal its core of self-interest and intention on the character's part. Wonder must have feet with which to walk the earth.

THE EVOLUTIONARY QUALITY OF LIFE

But before I leave this play it seems wise to say a few more words about the kind of dramatic impulse it represents, and one aspect of "Ibsenism" as a technique is the quickest path into that discussion. I have no vested interest in any one form—as the variety of forms I have used attests—but there is one element in Ibsen's method which I do not think ought to be overlooked, let alone dismissed as it so often is nowadays. If his plays, and his method, do nothing else they reveal the evolutionary quality of life. One is constantly aware, in watching his plays, of process, change, development. I think too many modern plays assume, so to speak, that their duty is merely to show the present countenance rather than to account for what happens. It is therefore wrong to imagine that because his first and sometimes his second acts devote so much time to a studied revelation of antecedent material, his view is static compared to our own. In truth, it is profoundly dynamic, for that enormous past was always heavily documented to the end that the present be comprehended with wholeness, as a moment in a flow of time, and not—as with so many modern plays—as a situation without roots. Indeed, even though I can myself reject other aspects of his work, it nevertheless presents barely and unadorned what I believe is the biggest single dramatic problem, namely, how to dramatize what has gone before. I say this not merely out of technical interest, but because dramatic characters, and the drama itself, can never hope to attain a maximum degree of consciousness unless they contain a viable unveiling of the contrast between past and present, and an awareness of the process by which the present has become what it is. And I say this, finally, because I take it as a truth that the end of drama is the creation of a higher consciousness and not merely a subjective attack upon the audience's nerves and feelings. What is precious in the Ibsen method is its insistence upon valid causation, and this cannot be dismissed as a wooden notion.

This is the "real" in Ibsen's realism for me, for he was, after all, as much a mystic as a realist. Which is simply to say that while there are mysteries in life which no amount of analyzing will reduce to reason, it is perfectly realistic to admit and even to proclaim that hiatus as a truth. But the problem is not to make complex what is essentially explainable; it is to make understandable what is complex without distorting and oversimplifying what cannot be explained. I think many of his devices are, in fact, quite arbitrary; that he betrays a Germanic ponderousness at times and a tendency to overprove what is quite clear in the first place. But we could do with more of his basic intention, which was to assert nothing he had not proved, and to cling always to the marvelous spectacle of life forcing one event out of the jaws of the preceding one and to reveal its elemental consistencies with surprise. In other words, I contrast his realism not with the lyrical, which I prize, but with sentimentality, which is always a leak in the dramatic dike. He sought to make a play as weighty and living a fact as the discovery of the steam engine or algebra. This can be scoffed away only at a price, and the price is a living drama.

Remembering
All My Sons

Arthur Miller

In *Timebends: A Life* (1987), Arthur Miller recalls
working on the first production of *All My Sons* with
Elia Kazan, who would later direct *Death of a Salesman* and Tennessee Williams's *A Streetcar Named
Desire*. Miller vividly depicts the tensions surrounding this make-or-break production, and Kazan's
unique approach to bringing out the hidden qualities
of both the actors and the script. In addition, he remembers the play's initial reception: Some influential critics greeted *All My Sons* with incomprehension, but audiences seemed to have no problem
understanding the play and were deeply moved.
Miller also responds to criticisms of *All My Sons*—
especially the accusation that it is too plot heavy and
that some of the scenes are contrived. Finally, the in-
tervening years and subsequent productions allowed
Miller to reflect on the universal nature of *All My
Sons*, and how it continues to speak to different cul-
tures and different historical circumstances.

The business at the moment was *All My Sons*.

The play had already run in New Haven and had shown
its impact, but [director] Elia Kazan continued rehearsing
sections of it every day even now, driving it to ever more intensified climaxes, working it like a piece of music that had
to be sustained here and hushed there. To keep the cast from
routinizing their characters' conflicts, he would stimulate
arguments among them by seeming to favor one over the
other, seeding little fungi of jealousy that made them com-
pete all over again for his affection. A small, compact man
who walked on the balls of his feet, he had the devil's energy
and knew how to pay attention to what the writer or his ac-

tors were trying to tell him; he could make each actor think
he was his closest friend. I think his method, if it can be
given so self-conscious a name, was to let the actors talk
themselves into a performance. Far more by insinuation
than by command, he allowed the actors to excite themselves with their own discoveries, which they would carry
back to him like children offering some found object to a
parent. And he respected rather than scoffed at actors' child-
ishness, knowing that it was not a grown-up occupation and
that the sources of their best inventions were in their earliest years. Instinctively, when he had something important to
tell an actor, he would huddle with him privately rather than
instruct before the others, sensing that anything that really
penetrates is always to some degree an embarrassment. . . .

Kazan came from close-knit people of intense feelings,
people of clannish propriety and competitiveness who knew
that no feeling is alien to man. His most reassuring side, for
me, was a natural tendency to seek out the organic and hew
to its demands. I believed by this time in a kind of biological
playwriting—nature abhors the superfluous, and whatever
does not actively contribute to the life of an organism is
sloughed off. This same predilection may be why Kazan was
not suited to Shakespeare and would have his difficulties
with Tennessee Williams,[1] who sometimes showed a weakness for verbal adornment for its own sake. In a play, as in
personal relations, Kazan knew that the making and the
breaking was done by the needs of people and not by their
avowals and disavowals. In the same spirit he listened to music, classical and jazz, seeking to experience what was naked
in it and expressive of the composer's secret outcry. He had
cast [actor] Ed Begley to play the father, Keller, in *All My Sons*
not only because Begley was a good actor (although not as
yet of great distinction) but because he was a reformed alcoholic and still carried the alcoholic's guilt. Keller is of course
a guilty man, although not an alcoholic; thus traits could be
matched while their causes were completely unrelated. . . .

Kazan was already a well-known but far from famous director at this time, still a year away from the mystique that
would come with his production of *A Streetcar Named Desire,* and I was almost totally new to the critics and newspa-

1. American playwright Tennessee Williams (1911–1983) was the author of more than
twenty full-length dramas, including *The Glass Menagerie* (1945) and *A Streetcar
Named Desire* (1947).

per theatrical columns, so despite very good Boston reviews, the enormous Colonial was never really filled. The Boston audience was still in a condition of what might be called stubborn spiritual stateliness, and it was hard for me to read their largely silent reactions. One tall and dignified man I saw standing in the lobby crowd at the intermission after the second-act curtain was quite visibly shaken by that climax, his eyes red with weeping. To his companion, who had asked what he thought of the play, he muttered through thin, barely moving lips, "I like it."

ALL MY SONS GREETED WITH INCOMPREHENSION

Something in the play seemed to have departed from tradition. It is possible that Mordecai Gorelik's set, a disarmingly sunny suburban house, as well as the designedly ordinary and sometimes jokey atmosphere of the first ten minutes, made the deepening threat of the remainder more frightening than people were culturally prepared for; this kind of placid American backyard was not ordinarily associated, at least in 1947, with murder and suicide. Ward Morehouse, the *New York Sun* drama critic, came up to see the play in New Haven and invited Kazan and me to have a drink with him so that he could ask us straight out, "What's it about?" Coming as it did a few months after the famous producer Herman Shumlin had said, "I don't understand your play," Morehouse's question mystified me, and I could only grope for an explanation of a story that, to me and Kazan at any rate, was absolutely clear. On top of this, in the coming weeks I would be asked by Jim Proctor, our press agent, to write a piece for the *Times* "to explain the play" and what I was after in writing it. Apart from the embarrassment of presuming to tell critics what to think, I was at a loss as to what needed elucidation.

MILLER'S RESPONSE TO CRITICISMS OF *ALL MY SONS*

After the play opened, one recurring criticism was that it was overly plotted, to the point of implausible coincidence. At a crucial moment, Annie produces a letter written to her during the war by her fiancé, the Kellers' son Larry, presumed dead; in the letter Larry declares his intention to commit suicide in his despair at his father's much publicized crime of selling defective plane parts to the army. With one stroke this proves that Larry is indeed dead, freeing Annie to marry

Chris, his brother, and at the same time that Joe Keller not only caused the deaths of anonymous soldiers but, in a manner he never imagined, that of his own son. If the appearance of this letter, logical though it might be, was too convenient for our tastes, I wondered what contemporary criticism would make of a play in which an infant, set out on a mountainside to die because it is predicted that he will murder his father, is rescued by a shepherd and then, some two decades later, gets into an argument with a total stranger whom he kills—and who just happens to be not only his father but the king whose place he proceeds to take, exactly as prophesied. If the myth behind *Oedipus*[2] allows us to stretch our commonsense judgment of its plausibility, the letter's appearance in *All My Sons* seems to me to spring out of Ann's character and situation and hence is far less difficult to accept than a naked stroke of fate. But I have wondered if the real issue is the return of the repressed, which both incidents symbolize. Whenever the hand of the distant past reaches out of its grave, it is always somehow absurd as well as amazing, and we tend to resist belief in it, for it seems rather magically to reveal some unreadable hidden order behind the amoral chaos of events as we rationally perceive them. But that emergence, of course, is the point of *All My Sons*—that there are times when things do indeed cohere.

THE UNIVERSALITY OF *ALL MY SONS*

In later years I began to think that perhaps some people had been disconcerted not by the story but by the play's implication that there could be something of a tragic nature to these recognizable suburban types, who, by extension, were capable of putting a whole world to a moral test, challenging the audience itself. This thought first crossed my mind in 1977 when I visited Jerusalem with my wife, Inge Morath, and saw a production of tremendous power. *All My Sons* had broken the record by then for length of run by a straight play in Israel, and the audience sat watching it with an intensifying terror that was quite palpable. On our right sat the president of Israel, Ephraim Katzir, on the left the prime minister, Yitzhak Rabin, who had arrived late because, as would be announced the next morning, he had just lost his post to Menachem Begin. At the end of the play the applause

2. *Oedipus Rex* was written by the Greek tragedian Sophocles (496 B.C.–406 B.C.).

seemed not to dispel an almost religious quality in the audience's attention, and I asked Rabin why he thought this was so. "Because this is a problem in Israel—boys are out there day and night dying in planes and on the ground, and back here people are making a lot of money. So it might as well be an Israeli play." I would have added that the authority of the play was enhanced by the performance of Hanna Marron, a very great actress whose leg had been blown off in a terrorist bombing of an El Al flight in Zurich in 1972, the year of the Munich Olympics massacre. Perhaps it was only my imagination, but her disfigurement as the result of war, which of course everyone knew about though her limp barely showed, seemed to add authenticity to Kate Keller's spiritual suffering in another war at a different time.

THE RICHNESS OF KATE KELLER'S ROLE

The play in this production was centered on Kate, the mother, which was an emphasis our original production had bypassed in favor of the father-son conflict. In London a few years later the same shift was made by Michael Blakemore directing Rosemary Harris in the role and Colin Blakely as the father, and it made me wonder whether it was a certain ambiguity in Kate Keller that had confused both Shumlin and the critic Morehouse. For while trying to put it out of her mind, she knows from the outset that her husband indeed shipped faulty plane engine elements to the army. Her guilty knowledge, so obdurately and menacingly suppressed, can be interpreted as her wish to deny her son's death but also, and perhaps even primarily, to take vengeance on her culpable husband by driving him psychically to his knees and ultimately to suicide. . . .

By spring the production was a fixture on Broadway and received the Drama Critics' Circle Award and a few others. After some weeks, realizing as I sat down to dinner with [wife] Mary in our Brooklyn Heights house that the Coronet Theatre was about to fill up yet again that evening with paying customers and that my words had a power beyond my mere self, I felt a certain threat along with the inevitable exhilaration. As a success I was occasionally greeted by people on the street with a glazed expression that was pleasant but made me feel unnervingly artificial. My identification with life's failures was being menaced by my fame, and this led me, a few weeks after the opening of *All My Sons*, to apply at the New York State Employment Service for any job available. I was sent out to a factory in Long Island City to stand all day assembling beer box dividers for the minimum wage. The grinding boredom and the unnaturalness of my pretense to anonymity soon drove me out of that place, but the question remained as to how to live without breaking contact with what theatre folk called the civilians, the ones in the audience who made the pants and filled the teeth. It was not merely a question of continuing to draw material from life but also a moral one. I had not yet read of [Russian novelist Leo] Tolstoy at the height of his renown spending days in a Moscow shop making shoes, but I shared his impulse.

CHAPTER 2

Themes

READINGS ON
ALL MY SONS

World War II and the Burden of Moral Responsibility in *All My Sons*

Sheila Huftel

First performed in 1947, *All My Sons* addressed an audience that had just emerged from the devastation of World War II. Sheila Huftel illustrates how *All My Sons* was inspired by Arthur Miller's interviews of combat soldiers during the war. She then proceeds to examine the extent to which the war colors the experiences of every character in the play. War veteran Chris Keller, for example, embodies the pain of committing oneself to high ideals of moral responsibility; it is Chris who must force his mother and father to confront their own moral blindness. The underlying principle of *All My Sons*, mediated through Chris Keller, is that the sacrifice of soldiers who lost their lives in World War II has to mean something. By the end of *All My Sons*, the "whole truth"—the clear relation between individuals and their broad moral obligations to society as a whole—comes to dominate the play. Huftel is the author of *Arthur Miller: The Burning Glass*.

"You have such a talent for ignoring things." This exasperated accusation is made by Chris in *All My Sons*, which, like Miller's adaptation of [Henrik Ibsen's] *An Enemy of the People*, deals with the clash between people who can and people who can not walk away from things. Both plays are about evasion and commitment, a wilful blindness and a need to see. Joe Keller and [*An Enemy of the People's*] Peter Stockmann can settle for an unprincipled practicality; Chris and Dr. Stockmann cannot.

Keller protests, in excuse, "Chris, a man can't be a Jesus in this world!" It is meaningless to Chris: without his commitment there would be no person left. Through Jim Bayliss, Miller shows what would have become of Chris had he followed the "practicality" urged on him. Jim was a doctor committed to research who imagined that he could give it up, accept a small-town practice, and not be lost. He is, in fact, destroyed far more deeply than Keller. "These private little revolutions always die. The compromise is always made . . . and now I live in the usual darkness; I can't find myself; and it is even hard sometimes to remember the kind of man I wanted to be." But for Miller compromise is not obligatory. . . .

The time of the play is just after the war and Chris embodies Miller's argument: "Everything was being destroyed, see, but it seemed to me that one new thing was being made. A kind of responsibility. Man for man. You understand me? To show that, to bring that onto the earth again like some kind of monument and everyone would feel it standing there, behind him, and it would make a difference to him. And then I came home and it was incredible. I—there was no meaning in it here; the whole thing to them was some kind of bus accident. I went to work for Dad and that rat-race again. I felt—what you said—ashamed somehow. Because nobody was changed at all. It seemed to make suckers out of a lot of guys. I felt all wrong to be alive, to open a bankbook, to drive the new car, to see the new refrigerator. I mean you can take those things out of a war, but when you drive that car you've got to know that it came out of the love a man can have for a man. You've got to be a little better because of that. Otherwise what you have is really loot, and there's blood on it."

Chris's belief seems to have grown out of a long line of experience. During the war Miller was asked to go round the camps and training centers of America to find the material for a true war film—only the facts, shorn of all fiction. Miller did not complete the script for *The Story of G.I. Joe,* but published what he had found in *Situation Normal. . . .* It is a sensitive book and through it Miller is driven by the need to define a belief that will make sense of the war. "Something besides horror must be proved, or only horror will remain." He was concerned with the individual behind the uniform, with the kind of world the soldier would be coming back to and what would happen if he was disappointed.

All My Sons and *Situation Normal*

Some aspects of the book seem to influence *All My Sons* and especially the full drawing of Watson.[1] Through his heroism in the Pacific Watson had been chosen for officers' training and sent home. He had found it hard to leave the island because he knew that "everybody had a right to go and wanted to."

His home town gave him a big demonstration and made him a hero. He talked with Miller mainly to ensure that there would be no mistakes in the film. "I liked it at the beginning," he told him, "but Jesus Christ, the real heroes never come back. They're the real ones. They're the only ones. Nobody's a hero if he can still breathe. . . . I mean I don't want to cheat so many dead men."

Watson spoke of the friendship out there, and his loyalty is reflected in Chris. When he tells Ann about the company he lost, he says in effect: "Friendship is the greatest thing out there. I mean real friendship, not because a guy can give you what you want. I tell you the truth: I would die for any one of the thirty or forty men out there just as easy as I'd flick out this match. I swear this is the truth. I don't expect you to believe it, but I swear it."

By contrast, Watson was alone in America. He was not doing well at the training camp and seemed not to have the intellectual ability for the courses. His dread was that if he failed he could not go home or back to the front. He did not know what he was going to do.

Miller understood the debt Watson felt, and in explaining him wondered what would become of the countless Watsons coming home to an America not conscious of nor fighting for its belief. "Half of him, in a sense, must die." He would have had a place in the struggle for a belief. "It would demand that part of his character which requires sharing. As it is, the company is gone and all that the company meant. He must wall himself from his fellow man, he must live only his own little life and do his own unimportant, unsatisfying job when he gets out of the Army. He must begin again the stale and deadly competition with his fellow men for rewards which now seem colorless, even if necessary for his survival. He is alone. Cut off from mankind and the great movement of mankind he was once part of. And the world is alien. . . ." Miller predicted that Watson "will be

1. A World War II combat veteran whom Miller interviewed for *Situation Normal*.

wondering why he went and why he is alive for the rest of his days. . . ." And this is the position Chris holds in the play. The difference is that through Chris, Miller defines the "idea" growing among the soldiers.

Miller wrote *Situation Normal . . .* when he was twenty-seven, and the book is rather like a young photograph. He remains concerned with how the world can be made less alien. . . . In *After the Fall* Quentin, outside the concentration camp, nails the idea behind *Situation Normal . . .* to one line: "And I without belief stand here disarmed."

ALL MY SONS' MORAL CONSTRUCT

The idea of *All My Sons* was in the air—almost, it must have seemed, tangible. The details of the plot were fact. Miller was told of a family in which the daughter discovered that her father had sold defective machinery to the Army, and she handed him over to the authorities. All Miller's plays are rooted in reality. It is part of his ambition to write plays for common-sense people, and ensures that his ideas will not float about like ghosts who have permanently lost their haunting-ground. His plays are built as though he were constructing skyscrapers, not scenes. He says in his Preface that he desired above all to write rationally, and adds: "I have always been in love with wonder, the wonder of how people got to be the way they are." Wonder, for Miller, is something essentially explicable, a logic of people and events caused by "the gradual and remorseless crush of factual and psychological conflict."

This is the basis of *All My Sons* and of all Miller's flesh-and-blood social drama. Keller killed twenty-one pilots during the war by shipping defective airplane parts, for which his partner was jailed. Nothing could be more clear cut; so far it is cardboard drama. But these people are involved in a forest of mutual and parallel relationships, and the play is so balanced that if Chris's relationship with his father is not fully established, half the play is lost. . . . Chris loves his parents and, although haunted by his brother's death, plans to marry Larry's fiancée, who is also the daughter of the jailed partner. The marriage is guaranteed to upset his mother because it confirms her son's death, something she cannot accept, sensing that if Larry is dead Keller is responsible. Chris is parallel to Frank, a practical opportunist, to George, the jailed man's son, and to Jim. He relates to every character in the play.

THE POWER OF RELATEDNESS

Miller carries this relatedness through from people to events; it is the foundation on which *All My Sons* is built. "Joe Keller's trouble . . . is not that he cannot tell right from wrong but that his cast of mind cannot admit that he, personally, has any viable connection with his world, his universe, or his society." Miller shies away from the obvious "crime" element in the play, the selling of defective airplane parts. That is too simple. It does not say enough. To Miller that would be the plot of a thriller, a meaningless kill-time. . . . In his Preface he defines what his play is about: "The fortress which *All My Sons* lays siege to is the fortress of unrelatedness. It is an assertion not so much of a morality in terms of right and wrong, but of the moral world's being such because men cannot walk away from certain of their deeds." Relatedness and responsibility. The central problem of the play is to bring the fact home to Joe Keller, to batter down the opaque-glass walls of his isolation. Miller is concerned with consciousness, not crime, and with bringing a man face to face with the consequences he has caused, forcing him to share in the results of his creation.

THE WORLD CHRIS KELLER HAS RETURNED TO

He is not a chess-playing dramatist, a manipulator of black and white pieces of wood hierarchically designed. Keller literally stands for the world that Chris has come back to, self-centered and unseeing. But Miller cares too much for his people to reduce them to ciphers; with Keller he wins his argument, but without crucifying the man. Keller is committed only to his family, and can see no further—nothing beyond that. Miller's drawing is always compassionate, and the man is so drawn that the general concepts of his son are outside the range of his understanding. His limitation is explained: "A heavy man of stolid mind and build . . . but the imprint of the machine-shop worker and boss still upon him. When he reads, when he speaks, when he listens, it is with the terrible concentration of the uneducated man for whom there is still wonder in many commonly known things, a man whose judgments must be dredged out of experience and a peasant-like common sense."

Keller illustrates Miller's belief that an idea is no guide to the man holding it until you know why he believes as he does. Keller's vulnerable position makes him appear more liberal than Ann when he, naturally, protests against her at-tack on her father: "I never believed in crucifying people." It is himself he is defending. Chris sees the facts; the man killed twenty-one pilots. There is nothing to add, and he drives Keller to his only defense: "A father is a father!" Miller adds a stage direction to deepen understanding of Keller; he has been particularly careful over him: "As though the out-burst revealed him, he looks about, wanting to retract it."

THE TRAGEDY OF SELF-REALIZATION

The insights Keller does have are nervelessly bludgeoning and accurate. His partner was "a little man . . . always scared of loud voices." Finally, this rock-solid egocentric is desperate and alone, alone in his version of what he has done. Baffled in the extreme, he still tries to blink facts by reaching for his family. His plea is a general one: "Then what do I do? Tell me, talk to me, what do I do?" Kate can-not help him, except to warn: "You want to live? You better figure out your life." Unrepentant, he argues that nothing is bigger than the family: "There's nothing he could do that I wouldn't forgive. Because he's my son. Because I'm his fa-ther and he's my son . . . and if there's something bigger than that I'll put a bullet in my head." In spite of the family, in spite of the generally accepted code of practicality—"Who worked for nothin' in that war?"—his self-justification breaks. It breaks on the realization that Larry deliberately crashed his plane, so making his father directly responsible for his death. And with final realization, Keller kills himself.

THE ROLE OF MINOR CHARACTERS

Miller draws his minor characters with a precision that tells you only what you need to know. This can make them ap-pear underdrawn until you notice how meticulously they re-veal themselves. Frank, who believes in fortunetelling by the stars, accuses Jim: "The trouble with you is, you don't *believe* in anything." Sue resents "living next door to the Holy Fam-ily. It makes me look like a bum, you understand?" George, Ann's brother, has a deeply felt sense of relationships: "I wanted to go to Dad and tell him you were going to be mar-ried. It seemed impossible not to tell him. He loved you so much . . . Annie, you don't know what was done to that man. You don't know what happened." This passionate concern for the individual is expressed in all Miller's plays.

THE WHOLE TRUTH

Miller's realism is the strength of his characters. The Kellers live on and are consoled by the heroism of their dead son, particularly the mother. Miller describes her as "a woman of uncontrolled inspirations and an overwhelming capacity for love." Kate is too sensitive to stare past facts like Keller. She wraps herself in dreams and from this phantom comfort tries to will Larry back to life by faith. Miller explores the reasons for Kate's delusion—her sickness, her being driven to clutch at mysticism and astrology—and at bottom discovers a genuine faith in a moral order. "Your brother's alive, darling, because if he's dead, your father killed him. Do you understand now? . . . God does not let a son be killed by his father."

Kate has to believe it. But when the dream breaks she protects Keller. Most often there is resilience in Miller's dreamers. The person comes through and they are not allowed to wander far from reality. . . .

The whole truth admits all the facts and irrelevancies that in life temper situations and characters; tragedy excludes them because they diminish its height and purity. The whole truth forbids Kate to languish in grief. She comes out into daylight and tries to prevent Chris from jailing Keller: "The war is over! Didn't you hear? It's over!" However moving, because coming from her, Chris reminds her that Larry didn't kill himself so that she and Keller could be "sorry."

KATE   What more can we be?

CHRIS   You can be better! Once and for all you can know there's a universe of people outside and you're responsible to it, and unless you know that, you threw away your son because that's why he died.

. . . In writing about Miller, people seem impelled to oversimplify him, arriving at a clear-cut half-man, half-truth. He denies the role thrust upon him of abstract moralist—talkative upon a peak in Darien. "*All My Sons* has often been called a moral play, but the concept of morality is not quite as purely ethical as it has been made to appear, nor is it so in the plays that follow." Put it this way: Miller is concerned with why people live the way they do; he is a builder with available materials rather than an architect hawking blueprints for an ideal house.

The Public and Private Environments of *All My Sons*

Tom Scanlan

In Arthur Miller's early work, the family functioned as a microcosm of the larger issues present in American society as a whole. For Tom Scanlan, this is certainly the case in *All My Sons:* The play undercuts Joe Keller's wish to find in his family refuge from the social consequences of his business decisions, and it strongly affirms the idea that the family is a part of the larger world. The desire to seek a safe haven from a heartless world is tempting, but through the medium of the Kellers, Miller wants to show that withdrawal from the social environment exacts a terrible cost. Scanlan is the author of *Family, Drama, and American Dreams.*

The story Miller tells in *All My Sons* concerns Joe Keller and the discovery that he shipped defective cylinder heads from his aircraft engine factory during World War II. The entire structure and movement of the play is aimed at this revelation and at Joe's belated recognition of the responsibility which he bears for his act. Miller has constructed a situation in which the nearly sensational social consequences of an act are easily and clearly identified. He dramatizes this strong situation by depicting the pressures of the Keller family relationships which drive the action toward revelation. The reaction of the two sons, Chris and Larry, to their father's crime generates the play's climax. As [critic] Dennis Welland has put it: "What concerns Miller here . . . is the impinging of the public issue on the private conscience and the domestic circle of the family."

Excerpted from *Family, Drama, and American Dreams,* by Tom Scanlan. Copyright © 1978 by Tom Scanlan. Reprinted with permission from Greenwood Publishing Group, Inc.

PUBLIC AND PRIVATE ENVIRONMENT

All My Sons takes place entirely in the Kellers' back yard,
which we quickly see is a center of neighborhood activity
with a constant stream of friends moving in and out. Thus
the action is set in a half-public, half-private environment,
one where the warmth, ease and love of family life is extended to encompass a larger area of society. In turn, the
neighbors know and have sympathy for the problems of the
Keller family. Here, then, is a family which seems to connect
with the outer world.

It is worthwhile to examine the method Miller has used
to tell the story of the Kellers. I have already noted that the
play is aimed at a single revelation and recognition. Miller
builds toward this crisis by starting out with a different
story, a rather complicated domestic crisis concerning
Chris's desire to marry Ann Deever. Kate Keller refuses to
recognize that her son Larry, missing in action three years
earlier, is dead and that his fiancée Ann is therefore free to
marry. In the midst of this family difficulty, a different subject begins to take shape during the long first act, one which
at first is apparently a gratuitous complication of the approaching crisis of marriage. Ann's father had been Joe
Keller's partner in their wartime factory and was convicted
for shipping faulty airplane parts, a charge of which Joe
was cleared. Here is the first hint of the ethic which is to
dominate the play—antisocial action by the individual produces horrifying public consequences which in turn react
on the individual. The realization that twenty-one pilots died
as a result of the defective equipment has turned neighbors
and his children against Steve Deever. As Joe Keller pleads
for sympathy for his former partner, Chris and Ann pro-
nounce their judgments on him.

> ANN, *a little shamed, but determined:* No, I've *never* written to
> him. Neither has my brother. To *Chris:* Say, do you feel this
> way [as your father does], too?
>
> CHRIS: He murdered twenty-one pilots.

At first this censure is applied at a distance, as it were, to
a person we do not see whose story seems only tangentially
related to the gathering crisis in family relations. Chris
threatens to leave the family business rather than give up
Ann, and Kate seems inflexibly determined to deny Larry's
death. But in the second act the theme of social responsibil-

ity becomes more directly a part of the domestic crisis with the arrival of George, Ann's brother. George has now come to believe his father's denial of guilt. He accuses Joe of being responsible for shipping faulty equipment; and he attempts to dissuade Ann from her marriage. His attack fails to move anyone except Kate. Driven to desperation by the determination of Ann and Chris to marry, she reveals that George's charge is true:

> MOTHER . . . To *Chris, but not facing them:* Your brother's alive, darling, because if he's dead, your father killed him. Do you understand me now? As long as you live, that boy is alive. God does not let a son be killed by his father. Now you see, don't you? Now you see.

THE FAMILY AS A MICROCOSM OF SOCIETY

Here Miller neatly brings his social ethic and his family situation together. For Kate the engagement of Chris and Ann means an admission of Larry's death, an admission which in her mind brings the consequences of her husband's act to bear on his own family. Joe is able to avoid this dilemma because his shrewd, practical outlook assures him his son never piloted a P-40 airplane. But Kate, a half-mystic, makes a symbolic connection between her son's death as a pilot and the deaths of those who actually flew P-40's. Despite her inability to hold any values other than family preservation and solidarity, despite her lack of understanding of the larger moral import of what her husband has done, she senses intuitively that her husband's act and her son's death bear some relation to each other.

In the structure of the play's dramatic action, as the domestic crisis comes to a head it brings with it a revelation of the consequences of a previous antisocial action. Each succeeding act of *All My Sons* is drastically shorter than the last, has sharper and more compact conflicts, and brings us closer to the crucial revelations. What Miller is saying is that one cannot escape into the family from the social consequences of one's actions. In *All My Sons* the family is part of a larger world and the structure of the dramatic action is designed to drive this lesson home.

Miller is not content with this revelation; the assertion of the family's connection with the outer world does not satisfy the question of moral responsibility, nor does it resolve the tensions set up in the Joe-Chris relationship. In the first acts

Joe is a remarkably passive character, considering the fact that he is central to the whole argument of the play. This is part of Miller's strategy, for he wishes to show that Joe is incapable of recognizing the consequences of his decision, and he wishes to heighten through contrast the drama of Joe's final action, his suicide. But in addition to these reasons of characterization and dramaturgy is the fact that Joe cannot see beyond his family and so has no sense of the crisis which is gathering about him. And when he is confronted by Chris, he is unable to admit his social responsibility because he does not think he has one. He justifies his actions in terms of his family:

> Chris, I did it for you, it was a chance and I took it for you. I'm sixty-one years old, when would I have another chance to make something for you? Sixty-one years old you don't get another chance, do ya?

Joe's role in the business world has no other meaning for him than as a provider for his family. He cannot see the consequences of his action in any other way. After his break with his son, Joe becomes antagonistic toward his neighbors and turns to Kate, whose great maternal warmth has always held the family together. "I thought I had a family here. What happened to my family?" Joe's highest, and indeed single, loyalty is to the family.

Chris believes in a loyalty that transcends the family, but he is unable to act on that belief until the final revelation, the disclosure of Larry's suicide in expiation of his father's sin. Chris is unwilling to act against his father since Joe's corruption has revealed the corruption of the whole business society, but Larry's letter convinces him of the necessity for action. It also convinces Joe, who can now begin to see his own responsibility:

> Sure, he was my son. But I think to him they were all my sons. And I guess they were, I guess they were.

Yet Joe is able to admit this only in retrospect, in his memory of a past action. He still cannot see it as the basis for a moral life, and so he kills himself as he said he would:

> I'm his father and he's my son, and if there's something bigger than that I'll put a bullet in my head.

THE COST OF FAMILY WITHDRAWAL FROM SOCIETY

In *All My Sons* Miller establishes the family as intimately connected with society, and he is brutally critical of the impulse to withdraw into the family. When loyalties to family and to society come into conflict, as they do in the Chris-Joe relationship, he demonstrates the necessity for family relationships to give way to a larger social responsibility.

The Keller family is one which disintegrates completely, yet out of this chaos Miller is attempting to bring his self-conscious character, Chris, into a moral and so human relationship with the world. Presumably, it is also supposed to be a "life-giving" relationship, to use Dennis Welland's term. But *All My Sons* does not clearly define this new alternative.

MAKING THE OUTSIDE WORLD A HOME

Few American dramatists have made the family as central to their work as Arthur Miller has. Not surprisingly, Miller believes that the great task of drama is to imaginatively establish a home for individuals in society as a whole as well as within their own family circles.

Up to this point I have been avoiding any question of content except that of the family relation as opposed to relations out in the world—social relations. Now I should like to make the bald statement that all plays we call great, let alone those we call serious, are ultimately involved with some aspect of a single problem. It is this: How may a man make of the outside world a home? How and in what ways must he struggle, what must he strive to change and overcome within himself and outside himself if he is to find the safety, the surroundings of love, the ease of soul, the sense of identity and honor which, evidently, all men have connected in their memories with the idea of family?

One ought to be suspicious of any attempt to boil down all the great themes to a single sentence, but this one—"How may a man make of the outside world a home?"—does bear watching as a clue to the inner life of the great plays. Its aptness is most evident in the modern repertoire; in fact, where it is not the very principle of the play at hand we do not take the play quite seriously. If, for instance, the struggle in *Death of a Salesman* were simply between father and son for recognition and forgiveness it would diminish in importance. But when it extends itself out of the family circle and into society, it broaches those questions of social status, social honor and recognition, which expand its vision and lift it out of the merely particular toward the fate of the generality of men.

Excerpted from Arthur Miller, "The Family in Modern Drama," in Robert A. Martin, ed., *The Theater Essays of Arthur Miller.* New York: Viking Press, 1978, pp. 73–74.

The morality of the play is measured by Larry's suicide, which is meant to be a symbol of ultimate commitment to one's social responsibilities. But it is life-giving only if one insists on the pun. Its dramatic effect is to save Chris's integrity by providing a model of extreme personal integrity for him to follow. Because commitment to one's individual integrity is a loyalty apart from family ties, Larry's suicide is associated with questions of social responsibility. He stands against wartime profiteering, which Joe justifies in terms of family prosperity. And Chris is motivated to take his father to the police by Larry's gesture. Still, Larry is a character we never see, one who does not appear in dramatic action before us, and our sense of the meaning of his life and death depends solely on a short suicide note. As a result, its revelation is more theatrical than dramatic.

More to the point, Chris needs such a model to follow because the society he lives in is, he feels, a false and corrupt one when compared to the wartime self-sacrifice he has seen. Banal common sense and immoral compromise must not win out as the neighbor, Jim Bayliss, wrongly predicts they will. Chris struggles to keep his "star of honesty." He is as involved with saving his individual soul as he is with gestures of social commitment. Larry's suicide, like the sacrifice of the soldiers for each other, is meant to provide Chris with a model which affirms a moral order larger than the family. It is intended as the dramatic counterbalance to Joe's suicide to establish the social theme Miller wishes to convey. But what is left dramatically inert is how Chris is to act after all this self-destruction. In the world of the play there is precious little room between innocence and death. One does not make the world a home by suicide.

A HUMAN COMMUNITY BEYOND THE FAMILY

Miller tries in *All My Sons* to use the family drama to illustrate the moral necessity of recognizing a human community beyond the family. He is not entirely successful. He establishes, through a highly crafted dramatic structure, the relentless destruction of the Keller family as the price they pay for refusing to recognize social responsibilities. This is the play's chief artistic success. But large elements of his theme of social responsibility remain only partly and indirectly realized in the action, for he is unable to define the way in which one was to *live* after the obstacle of family loyalty is removed. *All My Sons*, with its primary emphasis on the realistic psychology of familial relations, finally traps Miller within them. Once the Keller family relations are broken, he has no other dramatic materials to put in their place. Faced with the conundrum of the democratic family's isolation . . . Miller reaches outside the realistic style in his next play. What he retains of the materials and style of domestic drama is as important as what he discards.

The Challenge of Being Moral in a Corrupt World

Benjamin Nelson

Social obligation and commitment to the family unit exist in tension in *All My Sons*, and their eventual movement toward each other assures the play's thematic unity. Joe Keller's overdeveloped sense of family loyalty means he is morally expedient; on the other hand, Chris Keller's commitment to a sense of social responsibility is compromised by his decision to work for and believe in his father. With Joe Keller's final and rather belated awareness of his obligation to the larger world, and Chris Keller's discovery that he must sacrifice his father to authenticate his social ideals, Miller finally brings the two thematic poles of the play into harmony. Benjamin Nelson is the author of *Arthur Miller: Portrait of a Playwright*, from which the following article is excerpted.

The thematic image of *All My Sons* is a circle within a circle, the inner depicting the family unit, and the outer representing society, and the movement of the drama is concentric, with the two circles revolving in parallel orbits until they ultimately coalesce. . . .

The first act of *All My Sons* is a graphic example of Miller's attempt to particularize his theme by letting it emerge out of a specific communal context. Through leisurely pacing, casual conversations, and an accumulation of realistic detail, the act slowly and meticulously establishes a credible portrait of a typical mid-western town. . . . The secondary characters in *All My Sons* are integral to their play as they reinforce the domestic and communal insularity of the Kellers' environment. For it is precisely this insularity that provides the buffer between Joe Keller and his

Excerpted from *Arthur Miller: Portrait of a Playwright* (New York: David McKay, 1970) by Benjamin Nelson. Copyright © 1970 by Benjamin Nelson. Reprinted with permission from the author.

awareness of a relationship to a world beyond his front porch and backyard.

Perhaps the salient feature of the elder Keller is his affability. He is a pleasant man who enjoys the heartiness of a poker game with the boys, the relaxation of a Sunday afternoon in an easy chair, and the antics of the neighborhood children, a rather genial and somewhat bullish self-made man who is justifiably proud of his business and his imposing position in the community. Keenly aware of his lack of education and sophistication, he continually makes self-deprecating comments, but under the guise of this apparent humility, he cheerfully broadcasts his influence and connections.

Although he is intensely possessive toward his business, he is hardly a ruthless and scheming tycoon dominated by a lust for power. In fact he does not view the factory as an end in itself, but as the means by which he can give his family the security they presently enjoy, and enable his son to make the best possible life for himself.

Joe's ambitions for Chris are not entirely selfless. He wants the young man to have everything he can give him, but on Joe's terms. As a projection of his father, Chris must not only be as good as Joe, but greater. Nonetheless, to define this expectation as ruthless egotism masquerading under the guise of paternal love is to distort the entire relationship between these two men. Joe's hopes for his son contain the egocentricity of any father's unconscious desire to combat his mortality through the promise and potential of his children. The elder Keller would be appalled at any suggestion that his motivations toward his wife and son were in any way selfish or ambivalent.

JOE KELLER'S FLAWED VISION

This conscious and avowed dedication to his family manifests the flaw in Joe Keller's character which will eventually prove catastrophic. He is myopic. So preoccupied is he with the world of the inner circle that the outer world is a blur, and he is unable to recognize the external ramifications of what he considered a private act. This is why he can honestly refer to the deaths of twenty-one men as a 'mistake,' and why he is able to advise Ann that when her father is released from prison he should follow Joe's example and return to the town that has ostracized him.

'Till people play cards with him again,' Keller doggedly

assures her, 'and talk with him, and smile with him—you play cards with a man, you know he can't be a murderer. And the next time you write him I'd like you to tell him just what I said.'

A man simply cannot be a murderer if he is a good husband, loyal father, and all-around nice guy. In the inner circle he did not commit a crime; he was involved in an accident, and consequently the guilt he feels does not involve the twenty-one fliers nearly as much as it does the man whom he allowed to take all the blame for the 'mistake.'

Because Joe views his act as private, he is able to rationalize it in two ways. He can accept the lie that he never gave his partner the order to ship out the parts as necessary for the preservation of his family—an end which justifies any means for Joe. He can also visualize a wonderfully simple atonement. He will give Deever a job with the firm as soon as he is released; through his connections he will establish the man's son in a career; and finally he will take the daughter into his own family, thus making his partner's grandchildren heirs to the Keller legacy. A most reasonable and generous restoration. The consideration that atonement for twenty-one deaths is not quite as simple does not cross Joe's mind because they belong to the outer circle, which is still bewilderingly out of focus.

There is nothing extraordinary about Joe Keller's morality. Like his immediate neighbors and the community at large, he is a man with quite common, narrow loyalties, who might have lived a long, bland and complacent existence had he not become involved in an unusual situation. Ultimately it is not the monstrousness but the conventionality of Joe's outlook, actions, and rationalizations which provides the underlying horror of the play.

In two major confrontations with Chris, Joe expounds everything he believes in and stands for. At the end of the second act, when he is forced to admit his responsibility for sending out the defective cylinder heads, he begs his son to understand his reasons:

> What could I do! I'm in business, a man is in business; a hundred and twenty cracked, you're out of business; you got a process, the process don't work you're out of business; you don't know how to operate, your stuff is no good; they close you up, they tear up your contracts, what the hell's it to them? You lay forty years into a business and they knock you out in five minutes, what could I do, let them take forty years, let

them take my life away? I never thought they'd install them. I swear to God. I thought they'd stop 'em before anybody took off. . . . Chris, I did it for you. I'm sixty-one years old, when would I have another chance to make something for you? Sixty-one years old you don't get another chance, do ya?

In Joe Keller's eyes there is nothing dishonest in a plea to the two values upon which he has based his life: the worth of individual effort and the sanctity of family loyalty born of love. His second appeal extends beyond the individual and the family, but still is defined by the inner circle.

'You want me to go to jail?' he cries to his son. 'If you want me to go, say so.'

What's the matter, why can't you tell me. . . . I'll tell you why you can't say it. Because you know I don't belong there. . . . Who worked for nothin' in that war? When they work for nothin', I'll work for nothin'. Did they ship a gun or a truck outa Detroit before they got their price? Is that clean? It's dollars and cents, nickels and dimes; war and peace, it's nickels and dimes, what's clean? Half the goddam country is gotta go if I go! That's why you can't tell me.

FAMILY LOYALTY AND SOCIAL EXPEDIENCY

It is an appeal to a world beyond family but still lacking responsible human relationships, a world in which practicality has created its own particular brand of morality. Joe's problem is not an inability to differentiate between right and wrong. Although his family represents an absolute right for him, his preceding comments to Chris strongly emphasize his recognition that his actions in behalf of his wife and son were wrong. But he takes refuge in numbers, stressing that the only difference between his situation and thousands of similar ones lies in the gravity and the publicity of the consequences. Joe Keller does not claim moral rectitude for his actions: he claims family loyalty as an unshakable end, and social expediency for the less defensible means.

He is both victim and victimizer. His society has inculcated false values in him, and to the extent that these enable him to justify his behavior, society is partially responsible for his actions. But Joe has sinned against society also. Because of his intense and narrow allegiance to his family, he has committed a crime against the outer world. To protect those closest to him he has sacrificed others. The fascination of *All My Sons* lies precisely in its dramatization, not of good versus evil, but of a conflict between two forces, family and society, each of which is inherently good. The tragedy of Joe Keller's life is that a basically decent motivation has precipitated the catastrophe. The tragic irony of the play is that his crime against the outside world eventually becomes a crime against his own family as well, and in destroying those to whom he considers himself unrelated, he finally destroys those to whom he is most intensely bound.

THE ILLNESS OF UNRELATEDNESS

Although Joe Keller's crime is the sale of defective parts to the government, this crime is the consequence of the pervasive illness of unrelatedness. It is this bland but lethal disease that is so frightening for Miller because it plunges into jungle anarchy all civilization's attempts at order and meaning. And it is against this barrier of unrelatedness that Chris Keller hurls himself.

Chris is his father's antagonist, the individual who offers idealism as the possible antidote to Joe's expediency. It is an idealism contained in his explanation to Ann of what the war has meant to him. 'They weren't just men,' he says, referring to the soldiers in his platoon.

> One time it'd been raining several days and this kid came to me, and gave me his last pair of dry socks. Put them in my pocket. That's only a little thing . . . but . . . that's the kind of guys I had. They didn't die; they killed themselves for each other. . . . And I got an idea—watching them go down. Everything was being destroyed, see, but it seemed to me that one new thing was made. A kind of responsibility. Man for man . . . to show that, to bring that on earth again like some kind of monument and everyone would feel it standing there, behind him, and it would make a difference to him. And then I came home and it was incredible. I . . . there was no meaning in it here; the whole thing to them was a kind of a—bus accident. I went to work with Dad, and that rat-race again. I felt . . . ashamed somehow. Because nobody was changed at all. It seemed to make suckers out of a lot of guys.

With very few embellishments this is the speech in which the soldier Watson[1] tried to tell Miller what the war meant to him, and it is this idea—and his intense disillusionment at its failure to take root in his own home—which Chris flings in the teeth of his father's plea that he acted in the young veteran's behalf:

> For me! Where do you live, where have you come from? For

---

1. A combat soldier Miller interviewed for his book *Situation Normal* (1944).

me!—I was dying every day and you were killing my boys and you did it for me? What the hell do you think I was thinking of, the Goddam business? Is that as far as your mind can see, the business? What is that, the world—the business? What the hell do you mean you did it for me? Don't you have a country? Don't you live in the world?

Finally, in reply to his mother's question as to what more they can be, Chris extends his idealism to the perimeter of the outer circle.

'You can be better!' he exclaims. 'Once and for all you can know there's a universe of people outside and you're responsible to it, and unless you know that you threw away your son because that's why he died.'

CHRIS KELLER'S DIDACTIC ROLE

These ringing declarations have been cited by a number of critics to illustrate one apparently glaring weakness of *All My Sons*: a moral didacticism that bogs down the play in a sticky morass of righteousness. They have complained that Chris Keller is just too right, too good, and too insistent on his rectitude and goodness to be any reasonable facsimile of a human being. He has been labelled his author's moral pitchman, verbally clubbing an audience into dazed submission; and the playwright who had insisted on suppressing an idea unless 'it was literally forced out of a character's mouth,' has been sharply criticized for creating a character with a mouth that apparently needs very little forcing.

Although this criticism is valid, it must be sharply qualified, for the younger Keller is much more than a thematic megaphone through which the dramatist is trumpeting the play's message. He is an individual caught in a human conflict, and even though he often speaks for the author and his didacticism is not always controlled by the playwright, Chris certainly does not receive Miller's unconditional approval, nor does he warrant it. A great gulf looms between Chris's ideals and his actions, and anyone who fails to make this observation misses the crux of the son's relationship to his father.

CHRIS KELLER'S CONTRADICTIONS

Beneath the conflict of the two different systems of value Joe and Chris represent is the agonizing struggle between a father and a son, and although the ethical relationship between the two is clearly delineated, it is rooted in a complex personal involvement that defies any glib resolution. From an abstract moral perspective, Chris is Joe's prosecutor, the man who must show him his wrongness; but more pointedly, he is a son torn apart by the conflict between his devotion to his father and his concept of justice and humanity which that selfsame parent has outraged. Consequently, while they herald his idealism, Chris's exhortations ultimately exhibit his ineffectuality as prosecutor. The louder he declaims, the more he signals his inability to become the disinterested moral voice he is often accused of being.

Chris cannot be the impartial prosecutor for three basic reasons. . . . [Firstly,] he is a son overwhelmed by the revelation of paternal guilt. All his life his view of his father has been so magnified that Joe's sins are not proof of human frailty, but evidence of the collapse of a deity.

'I never saw you as a man,' Chris exclaims in horror when the elder Keller begs for understanding. 'I saw you as my father.'

In this context, 'father' means the personification of goodness and infallibility, and when this image collapses Chris can only feel the terrible betrayal of a childhood faith. Each man bears the burden of responsibility—Joe for casting himself in a role he cannot fulfill, and Chris for adamantly maintaining his adolescent adoration of an impossible idol—and each pays for the dichotomy between reality and the illusion he has fostered.

Secondly, Chris cannot shake the realization that whatever his father did, he did for him. Thus, despite all his protestations, he knows that circumstance has made him a dominant factor in his father's degradation, and this knowledge continually complicates his desperate attempts to separate Joe's actions from their motivations.

Thirdly, and most significantly, Chris's shame and rage are not directed solely against his father; they are also aimed at himself. For all his lip service to humanitarian ideals, Chris is torn by guilt at what he considers to be his sellout to the same society and values he detests. And his shame is intensified because in working for his father he must suppress any suspicion he has held since the older man's arraignment. Thus, although sincerely felt, Chris's idealism is tinged with a hollowness that an unsympathetic neighbor labels hypocrisy. . . .

'What must I do, Jesus God, what must I do?' he cries at the end of the second act; and at the conclusion of the play the tune has not substantially changed.

'I can't look at you this way,' he complains to Joe, and then shamefully adds: 'I can't look at myself.'

His final words, following his father's suicide, further delineate his paralysis:

'Mother, I didn't mean to . . .' he exclaims, his voice trailing off.

The idealistic veteran meant to, but the son, torn between duty and love, was never able to enact the ultimate and dreadful condemnation of his father. Only the older man's death can break the stalemate, and even then Chris's mother must literally push him out of the stricken house to save him. . . .

JOE KELLER'S FINAL AWARENESS

Ironically the man who most fully commits himself to Chris's idealism is not the younger Keller but the man who violated every concept of it. It is Joe Keller who arrives at a genuine recognition of the meaning of his crime, and then firmly translates his awareness into action. Significantly, his illumination is not the result of Chris's harangues but of the discovery of his responsibility for his other son's death. Chris has brought Joe to the point of comprehension, but the older man's moral perspective is still blurred. As his son hammers at his unrelatedness, Joe only knows that his family is beginning to disintegrate in spite of his desperate efforts to hold it together, and even when his wife tries to explain that for Chris there 'is something bigger than the family,' Joe still cannot understand.

'Nothin's bigger than that,' he insists defiantly. 'I'm his father and he's my son, and if there's something bigger than that I'll put a bullet in my head!'. . .

Not until this last bastion of his defense is demolished does Joe's vision freeze into clear and terrible focus. With his realization that like Chris's world, Larry's also extended far beyond 'the building line,' Joe finally understands how circumscribed his own has been, and how his narrow commitment to it has caused him to defile the one outside. When his wife pleads with him not to surrender to the authorities, by attempting to convince him that Larry would never have advocated such a move, Joe gazes solemnly at the letter from his son.

'Then what is this if it isn't telling me?' he replies. 'Sure he was my son. But I think to him they were all my sons. And I guess they were, I guess they were.'

No wonder Miller selected this line when he revised the play's title. Emerging as it does from the morass of Joe's defensive declarations and groping questions, and set against the impassioned and strained rhetoric of Chris's exhortations, its simple and dignified finality poignantly testifies to its speaker's profound self-awareness and relatedness to a world he only dimly knew existed.

Surface Meanings and Deeper Implications

Ramesh K. Srivastava

The opening stage directions of *All My Sons* present a prosperous and sheltered suburban home, yet what follows exposes the secrets that lie hidden behind this veil of respectability. According to Ramesh K. Srivastava, this tension between the visible and the submerged is the force that drives *All My Sons*, from symbols such as the apple tree and the storm that destroys it to the fictional delusions the characters create in order to survive the truth. Srivastava is a professor of English at Guru Nanek Dev University in India. He has published works on Ernest Hemingway, Anita Desai, and Henry David Thoreau.

The significance of any work of art lies not only in the manifest but also in the hidden, not so much in what appears on the surface as in what lies underneath. Arthur Miller himself refers to the need "to prove the connections between the present and the past, between events and moral consequences, between the manifest and the hidden", thereby suggesting that certain incidents, objects, images, characters and dialogues in *All My Sons* could have both surface meaning and deeper implications, and this hints at the possible use of symbols and irony. It is by the juxtaposition of both the visible and the submerged, the seen and the unseen, that Miller makes the play interesting and valuable both to the common reader and the serious literary critic.

SURFACES AND DEPTHS

The two aspects of the world reflected in *All My Sons* begin to be clear with the stage directions. The house was constructed in the 1920s but now has been "nicely painted" and "looks" tight and comfortable, ironically implying that it is not really so. With Joe Keller and Kate going in opposite directions, with Larry dead and Kate working against Chris on the question of marriage—the house can only have the appearance of a family in it but with family spirit missing.

Joe Keller, a business man of sixty-one, is the head of the family consisting of his wife Kate and son Chris. Though he gives the impression of a "boss", having perfect control over things, in reality he is not even his own master and shoots himself when accused of sacrificing human beings, including his own son, for money. Equipped with a "peasant-like commonsense" but devoid of a sharp critical faculty and good education, Joe Keller does not understand why everyone gets educated. Being unimaginative, he fails to differentiate between the manifest and the hidden, giving importance to the former disproportionate to its value and turning a blind eye to the latter. He is "genuinely unable to foresee the public consequences of a private act." Arthur Miller believes that Joe's problem is not due to the absence of a faculty to discriminate between right and wrong, "but that his cast of mind cannot admit that he, personally, has any viable connection with his world, his universe, or his society." [Critic] Barry Gross also considers Joe Keller "guilty of an anti-social crime not out of intent but out of ignorance; his is a crime of omission, not of commission."

What is common in the above views is that Joe Keller has not done the crime wilfully after a careful examination of its possible dreadful consequences. He made his decision under the pressure of circumstances. What impelled him was fear of losing his business for the success of which he had struggled for forty years. He asks his son: "You lay forty years into a business and they knock you out in five minutes, what could I do, let them take forty years, let them take my life away?" Joe was under the impression that somehow the installation of defective cylinder heads would be stopped. Since he cannot envision a world beyond his family, he cannot relate his actions to their logical consequences in a far-off world, and thus his is the crime of "unrelatedness". And yet, as happens with many inadequately endowed human beings, he considers himself more intelligent than others, not realising that others do see behind his mask even if they don't say so, though revealing in their eyes that he is a criminal. How poor his commonsense is has been proved by the fact that he threw a bag of potatoes in the pail, mistaking it for a bag of garbage, in the same way as he had mistaken and thrown out a bag of onions. It is this failure of his critical faculty, even commonsense, which had led him to advise Steve Deever, a partner in the factory, to weld and paint the cracked cylinder heads and to send them to the Army Air Force, not realising that such an act might result in the crashing of twenty-one P-40s in Australia and the deaths of their pilots. Though Joe and his partner Steve were convicted in the court, subsequently Joe's exoneration from the crime in the appeal, and the confirmation of the verdict in the case of Steve, manifestly prove the former to be innocent, and he prefers to believe it, not knowing that without being guided by such judgements of the court, the people with their penetrating sight look below the surface, go deep and know who the real culprit is. Joe Keller rationalises that his activities have been for his sons even though he himself is not "brainy". He wanted to do something for them in his life but instead ended up by killing one of his own sons along with twenty-one pilots whom he later calls "all my sons".

JOE KELLER'S FICTIONAL UNIVERSE

Joe Keller also maintains certain fictions—believing in things which exist only in the manifest, not in reality. One such fiction is that of the existence of a jail in the basement of his house as he swears to the eight-year-old Bert, though the latter never finds it. Joe also shows him an "arresting gun", though here again Bert is convinced that no one is ever arrested and put in jail. Even Kate feels unhappy over the fiction of the jail maintained by Joe and she vehemently denies its existence. Probably, the existence of the jail is a symbol of his own guilt. Another fiction is that the money he has earned is good and that there is nothing wrong with it. Ann is also convinced and tries to persuade Chris that Joe has earned his money honestly by putting hundreds of planes in the air and Chris should be proud of it. If there was any person responsible for supplying cracked cylinder heads to the Army Air Force and of earning dishonest money, it was her father, Steve, she maintains, and not Joe. Connected with this is yet another fiction that Joe was suffering from flu on the day when the cracked cylinder heads were being shipped, though this is unwittingly exposed by Kate when she tells George that Joe had never fallen ill for many years. This fiction is believed in by Ann to such an extent that she refuses to show any consideration to her father, declines to write a letter to him, and gets upset when Joe wants her to be considerate to her father. However, Chris is not proud of his father's money because he suspects that his father was in some way responsible for causing many deaths, even if his guilt "bears the facade of respectability and success". He says, "I was made yellow in this house because I suspected my father and I did nothing about it." Joe's proposal of changing the name of his concern to his son's is turned down by the latter. He assures the suspecting Chris that what he has made is "good money, there's nothing wrong with that money", but the reader is well aware that this too is a well-maintained fiction even if most people believe it. While Chris suspects his father, Ann believes in the fiction completely largely because of her faith in Chris, who would "never take five cents out of that plant if there was anything wrong with it". She resents the hint put forward by Sue that Joe has been doing something wrong, while Sue, in return, resentfully pronounces them "the Holy family".

THE FICTION OF THE HOLY FAMILY

Yet another fiction of Joe Keller is that he has a loving family and all his activities, including the shady ones, have been directed for the happiness of his family—his wife and his sons—while in reality the family has been disintegrating because of his dubious role in the business. When Kate too refuses to listen to him, the fiction of having a family begins to be clear to him and he cries in exasperation, "What am I, a stranger? I thought I had a family here. What happened to my family?" In reality, his family is not based on mutual consideration, respect and feelings of well-being; all he has is his business. For the sake of money, he deceives his partner, sells cracked cylinder heads which have a disastrous consequence and drives his son Larry to commit suicide, even though maintaining on the surface that "I never believed in crucifying people". Once Chris comes to know clearly what was hidden from him so far about his father's inhuman activities, he feels humiliated by what the people must be thinking of his father's business and wants to run away from the whole thing. This shocks Joe because he feels that all he did in the business was for his children, placing the family above everything else, saying "Nothin' is bigger". The irony is that it is this very business which kills Larry, and drives Joe's wife Kate crazy. Hence, in reality he has no family in its broad sense in which each member is considerate to the others and is prepared to sacrifice everything for the well-being, dignity and honour of other members. Once this fact dawns upon him he commits suicide. Chris, on the contrary, believes that the values, the nation, and the lives of others are greater than the family. Since Joe's dishonest activities were done for his son and wife, he expects to be forgiven by them. He says, "I'm his father and he's my son, and if there is something bigger than that I'll put a bullet in my head!" It is only towards the end that Joe can understand the hidden beyond the manifest, that not only Larry but all the pilots who flew the planes and got killed were his sons. It is this ideal which Chris attempts to explain to his Mother, "Once and for all you can know there's a universe of people outside and you're responsible to it, and unless you know that, you threw away your son because that's why he died". When the realisation comes to Joe that the concept of family which he has been nurturing all his life is not the right one, that all along he has been too narrow in his beliefs, he feels quite uneasy. To accept this idea would be to negate all the activities and beliefs of his lifetime and that would be too great a loss for him. Not to accept it would be to lose even his second son Chris, who has threatened to go away from his father. It is here and in this sense that the public issues, as [critic Darshan] Maini maintains, "impinging on individual consciences have, so to speak, thrown filial relations out of gear, and put instinctive loyalties and pieties to a severe moral test". Even though Joe comes to realise the significance of Chris's concept of responsibility for one's actions, he is conscious of the fact that after spending so many years in the manifest world of innocence, it would be too difficult for him to live as a criminal. He tells Chris: "It's your money, that's not my money. I'm a dead man, I'm an old dead man, nothing's mine". The statement on the surface seems to be incorrect because Joe is neither dead nor does the money belong to Chris. It appears to be the typical outburst of an old man who is hinting at the possibility of his death in the future and of his son inheriting the property. This simple statement, however, has within it the potentiality of dramatic irony, as if his words were pointing to the fact that he was going to commit suicide. When he does so after a short time, the statement turns out to be ironically true.

KATE KELLER'S DELUSIONS

As Joe Keller has been maintaining the fictions of jail, of family, and of good money, his wife Kate has been maintaining the fictions of Larry being alive and of considering Ann as his girl-friend. Even though repeatedly assured by others, including Ann, that her son Larry is dead, Kate refuses to believe it. She does not know that Joe and Chris know of Larry's death, but that they let her believe in the manifest. The make-believe world remains there for three years and she continues to wait for his return. Joe himself does not object to Chris's marriage with Ann, partly because he is aware of Larry's death and also because marriage in America is largely the concern of the persons who are directly involved, not of their parents. But Joe must be aware of Kate's belief that Larry is alive and as such he asks Chris to make sure that his mother does not object. Believing Larry to be alive, Kate feels that Chris has no right over his girl-friend Ann. Associated with this is another of Kate's beliefs in the manifest, that Ann has not married anyone for over three years because she has been mourning the disappearance of Larry and waiting for him to return; otherwise she could have found any one of so many young men in New York to marry. Considering Ann faithful as a rock, Kate can think of nothing except that Ann has all along been waiting for Larry. But this well-maintained fiction of Kate's collapses at the end when Ann shows her readiness to marry Chris. Even Joe wants the fiction to be maintained, for otherwise the marriage of Chris and Ann would mean pronouncing Larry dead. Of course, Chris does not believe in this fiction. Instead of living in the make-believe worlds of his father and mother at the cost of his own existence, he would rather leave his father's business and go somewhere else so that he could marry Ann and live a happy married life. Towards the end of the play one comes to realise that the beliefs of Kate about Larry are not true. She has reason for believing in and maintaining the fiction because she knows that Joe was responsible for sending the defective cylinder heads. To accept Chris's marriage with Larry's girl would mean accepting Larry's death and, as a corollary, that her husband Joe had caused it. She says, "God does not let a son be killed by his father", and implies by this that the fact of Joe being a murderer hidden from others is so unpalatable that she would prefer to believe in the manifest image of Joe's innocence.

CHRIS KELLER'S INVOLVEMENT IN MANIFEST INNOCENCE

Chris Keller has also been accepting the manifest for some time. To a certain extent he is aware of Larry's death and suspects the business activities of Joe, but he is not quite sure as to what extent the latter was responsible for Larry's death. He has loved Ann but without letting her know for nearly two years and revealed it to her only when she was on the point of marrying someone else. Even his way of kissing her shows his fears. Chris's association with his father is no different. He maintains that his father is "a great guy" though he knows he is not so in reality. Larry's letter to Ann, written on the eve of his disappearance, makes it clear beyond doubt how Joe had been responsible for supplying defective cylinder heads to the Army Air Force which resulted in the deaths of twenty-one pilots. Chris debates the question of sending his father to jail, which on the manifest level seems the only way to ease his conscience. Chris, who had all along half-suspected it to be true, is now terribly shocked, surprising his mother who "always had the feeling that in the back of his head, Chris . . . almost knew". He goes out, not to watch the star of his honesty go out but, as [critic] Barry Gross feels, the fading of "the star of his image of himself as honest, not of the fact of his innocence which he has persisted in believing. It is not that he *will* compromise himself, it is that he *has* compromised himself, and now he can no longer deny it." After spending several hours outside his house, Chris Keller has a deeper awareness of things. If he sends his father to jail, would it bring about any change? After discussing the matter with Ann, he comes to the conclusion that by such an act he would change nothing. . . .

THE FUNCTION OF SYMBOLS IN THE PLAY

The relationship between the manifest and the hidden is also seen in the use of certain objects as symbols. One such object is the apple tree. As one begins reading the play, it becomes clear even in the stage directions that Miller wishes to make it a symbol. According to the stage directions, there stands in the left corner "the four-foot-high stump of a slender apple tree whose upper trunk and branches lie toppled besides it, fruit still clinging to its branches". The tree has been blown down by the wind and in its fallen state, it could be a symbol of Larry Keller really dead but sustained by the absence of evidence and prevalence of rumours. [Critic Santosh] Bhatia considers the broken apple tree "not only suggestive of Larry's premature death but [it] also forebodes the final catastrophe that is in the offing." There are many details which point in this direction. Frank connects Larry with the tree, saying, "Larry was born in August. He'd been twenty-seven this month. And his tree blown down". In the month of Larry's birth, Kate sees everything connected with him—his tree, his Ann and his gloves. In her dream she associates the tree with Larry and the roaring of the wind with the firing of his engine. When Larry was flying a plane, there was noise and the tree fell. In this way, in Kate's dream two images of Larry flying a plane and the falling of the tree are merged. Successive details confirm this relationship. Kate cried when she had noticed the tree falling and she also cries when she hears of Larry's death, whom she had been considering alive. It is the wind that breaks the tree and it is in the air that Larry disappears with his plane. Both are considered accidents. The storm that breaks the tree can be a symbol of the storm that rips apart the family after Ann gives the letter regarding Larry's death to his parents, driving the last nail into the fiction of the possible reappearance of Larry. When Ann goes to sleep in Larry's room, his memorial breaks into pieces. The tree fell down the same night as Ann came. Even Kate realises that "there are meanings in such" accidents.

A set of objects, mutually related, used repeatedly in the play and with ironical significance are the weather forecast and Larry's horoscope. Joe Keller reads the weather forecast in the newspaper but Dr. Jim Bayliss contradicts it by saying that because the paper has predicted rain, it would not rain, implying that paper predictions are manifestly good but really misleading. Connected with the weather forecast is the prediction based on Larry's horoscope which is only as good as a paper prediction—that is, it makes people believe in the manifest world even if what is hidden could ironically be contrary to it. Frank works on Larry's horoscope with a view to find out if November the twenty-fifth was a favourable day for Larry because he was reported missing on that day, and if the day were to be found favourable, "it would be practically impossible for him to have died on his favourable day". Frank even goes to the extent of saying, "Somewhere in this world your brother is alive". He lays a million to one odds of a man dying on his favourable day. Besides, the day was good for marriage, not for death. It is ironical that the predictions are being made by Frank whom Dr. Jim Bayliss considers "completely out of his mind", and whose observations are characterised by Chris as "junk". It is the same Frank whom Sue calls a dog and makes fun of him by calling him Thomas Edison when he fixes a toaster. At the end of the play, the hidden and the manifest change places and contrary to Frank's predictions, Larry is found to be dead.

MILLER'S REALISM IS SOPHISTICATED AND MULTILAYERED

Arthur Miller considers *All My Sons* a realistic play. However, realism is presented not in a very straightforward manner but through various layers which, on being peeled away one by one, give way to the hidden meaning. By bringing together the two worlds of the manifest and the hidden, Miller creates suspense for the reader whose anxieties are aroused and satisfied, alternatively. It not only helps in maintaining a continuing interest in the play but adds the element of wonder, for Miller has "always been in love with wonder, the wonder of how things and people got to be what they are." It is as if the reader has passed through the labyrinthine passages of the manifest to reach the hidden and in the process has gained experience about the world— an experience, to use Miller's words, "which widens their awareness of connection—the filaments to the past and the future which lie concealed in life."

Since the world itself operates on the levels of appearance and reality, by bringing together the two worlds of the manifest and the hidden, Miller creates a realistic world as it exists today and which cannot be taken at its face value. The dichotomy between things said and done, between what the people appear to be and what they are, characterises the modern world. The main interest of the play comes from the juxtaposition of these paradoxical aspects of the world; Joe Keller's innocence and Steve Deever's crime, Frank Lubey's astrological prediction and Kate Keller's obsessive denials of Larry's death, Ann's belief in Steve's crime and Chris's faith in his father's innocence do not, as they seem to, constitute the idealistic worlds; they only conceal the shocking reality.

Since Arthur Miller believes in conveying ideas, even morals, through his plays, he seems to be cautioning the reader in *All My Sons* that if a tragedy is to be averted in life, the world of the manifest should not be perpetuated at the cost of the hidden, that reality can be hidden only for a short time, not for ever, and that a person who closes his eyes to the stark realities of life or the consequences of his actions, as do Joe and Kate, is likely to end up tragically.

The Mystery of the Human Heart

Arvin R. Wells

All My Sons has long been viewed primarily as a social drama, the underlying theme being that an individual must recognize his or her moral obligation to
the larger world. However, Arvin R. Wells pays
homage to the play's psychological richness. Noting
the complexity of human motivation as it is expressed through Joe Keller, and the extent to which
the immense shadow of guilt determines the actions
of the Keller family, Wells concludes that *All My
Sons* strikes a perfect balance in representing both
social and psychological concerns. Wells is a professor of English at Ohio University.

Looked at superficially, Arthur Miller's *All My Sons* may appear to be simply a social thesis play. Such classification—a
valid one if severely qualified—is suggested both by the
timeliness of the story and by the presence of considerable
overt social criticism. The story itself is obviously calculated
to engage the so-called social conscience. Stated in the simplest terms, the play dramatizes the process by which Joe
Keller, a small manufacturer, is forced to accept individual
social responsibility and, consequently, to accept his personal guilt for having sold, on one occasion during World
War II, fatally defective airplane parts to the government.

A BALANCED CONCEPT OF LIFE

However, while this bare-bone synopsis is essentially accurate, it does, in fact, do violence to the actual complexity
of the play. In his well-known essay "Tragedy and the Common Man," Miller comments,

> . . . Our lack of tragedy may be partially accounted for by the
> turn which modern literature has taken toward the purely
> psychiatric, or purely sociological. . . . From neither of these

Reprinted from "The Living and the Dead in *All My Sons*," by Arvin R. Wells, *Modern
Drama*, May 1964. Reprinted with permission from *Modern Drama*.

views can tragedy derive, simply because neither represents a balanced concept of life.

What is reflected here is Miller's own careful avoidance of the "purely" this or that. And it might similarly be said that no satisfactory understanding of Miller's *All My Sons* may be derived from a criticism which commits itself to a "purely" or even predominantly sociological or psychiatric view. The sociological view is particularly limiting in that it carries with it the temptation to approach the dramatic action from the level of broad socio-cultural generalizations and, consequently, to oversimplify character and action and, stumbling among subtleties of characterization, to accuse the playwright of a confusion of values which belongs appropriately to the characters in their situations.

THE COMPLEXITY OF HUMAN MOTIVATION

Actually, like most of Miller's plays, *All My Sons* demands of the reader an awareness of the deviousness of human motivation, an understanding of the way in which a man's best qualities may be involved in his worst actions and cheapest ideas, and, in general, a peculiarly fine perception of cause and effect. Nowhere is it suggested that the social realities and attitudes that are brought within the critical focus of the play can be honestly considered outside of some such context of human aspirations and weaknesses as is provided by the play; and nowhere is it suggested that the characters are or can be judged strictly on the basis of some simple social ethic or ideal that might be deduced from the action. The characters do not simply reflect the values and attitudes of a particular society; they use those values and attitudes in their attempt to realize themselves. And it is these characteristics that give *All My Sons*, and other Miller plays, a density of texture so much greater than that of the typical social thesis play, which seeks not only to direct but to facilitate ethical judgments upon matters of topical importance.

For most of us there is no difficulty in assenting to the abstract proposition which Chris puts to his mother at the end of the play:

> You can be better! Once and for all you can know now that the whole earth comes through those fences; there's a universe outside and you're responsible to it.

And there is no problem either in giving general intellectual assent to the morality of brotherhood for which Chris speaks. There is, however, considerable difficulty in assenting to the actual situation at the end of the play, in accepting it as a simple triumph of right over wrong. For the play in its entirety makes clear that Joe Keller has committed his crimes not out of cowardice, callousness, or pure self-interest, but out of a too-exclusive regard for real though limited values, and that Chris, the idealist, is far from acting disinterestedly as he harrows his father to repentance.

Joe Keller is a successful small manufacturer, but he is also "a man whose judgment must be dredged out of experience and a peasant-like common sense." Like many uneducated, self-made men, he has no capacity for abstract considerations; whatever is not personal or at least immediate has no reality for him. He has the peasant's insular loyalty to family which excludes more generalized responsibility to society at large or to mankind in general. At the moment of decision, when his business seemed threatened, the question for him was not basically one of profit and loss; what concerned him was a conflict of responsibilities—his responsibility to his family, particularly his sons to whom the business was to be a legacy of security and joy, versus his responsibility to the unknown men, engaged in the social action of war, who might as a remote consequence suffer for his dishonesty. For such a man as Joe Keller such a conflict could scarcely exist and, given its existence, could have only one probable resolution.

JOE KELLER'S INSULARITY AND FEARS

When the worst imaginable consequence follows—twenty-two pilots killed in Australia—Keller is nonetheless able to presume upon his innocence as established before the law. For in his ethical insularity—an insularity stressed in the play by the hedged-in backyard setting—he is safe from any serious assault of conscience so long as he can believe that the family is the most important thing and that what is done in the name of the family has its own justification. Yet, he is not perfectly secure within his sanctuary. His apparently thick skin has its sensitive spots: in his unwillingness to oppose his wife's unhealthy refusal to accept her son Larry's death, in his protest against Ann Deever's rejection of her father, in his insistence that he does not believe in "crucifying a man," and in his insistence that Chris should use what he, the father, has earned, "with joy . . . without shame . . . with joy," he betrays a deep-seated fear. His appeal on behalf of [Steve] Deever (Act 1) is in fact, partly a covert appeal on his own behalf, an appeal for merciful understanding called forth by the shocked realization that some considerations may override and even destroy the ties of family upon which his own security rests.

CHRIS AND KATE'S PSYCHOLOGICAL WOUNDS

It is Chris Keller who, in reaching out for love and a life of his own, first undermines and then destroys this security altogether. Chris has brought out of the war an idealistic morality of brotherhood based on what he has seen of mutual self-sacrifice among the men whom he commanded. But he has not survived the war unwounded; he bears a still festering psychological wound, a sense of inadequacy and guilt. He has survived to enjoy the fruits of a wartime economy, and he fears that in enjoying them he becomes unworthy, condemned by his own idealism. Even his love for Ann Deever, the sweetheart of his dead brother, has seemed to him a guilty desire to take advantage of the dead to whom he somehow owes his life.

As the play opens, however, he has decided to assert himself, to claim the things in life and the position in life which he feels should rightfully be his, and as the initial step he has invited Ann to his family home. His decision brings him into immediate conflict with his mother, Kate Keller, who looks upon the possible marriage between Chris and Ann as a public confirmation of Larry's death. At first Joe Keller seems only peripherally involved in this conflict; his attempt to evade Chris's demand that Kate be forced to accept Larry's death carries only ambiguous suggestions of insecurity. However, at the end of Act II, Kate, emotionally exhausted by the fruitless effort to use George Deever's accusations as a means of driving out Ann, and opposed for the first time by the declared disbelief of both husband and son, breaks down and reveals the actual basis of her refusal: if Chris lets Larry go, then he must let his father go as well. What is revealed here is that Kate is fundamentally like her husband; only what is personal or immediate is real for her. If Larry is alive, then, in a sense, the war has no reality, and Joe's crimes do not mean anything; their consequences are merely distant echoes in an unreal world. But if Larry is dead, then the war is real, and Joe is guilty of murder, even, by an act of association, guilty of murdering his own son. Her own desperate need to reject Larry's death against all odds and upon whatever flimsy scrap of hope has been the reflex of her need to defend her relation to her husband against whatever in herself might be outraged by the truth about him. Actually, however, Kate has "an overwhelming capacity for love" and an ultimate commitment to the living which makes it possible for her to "let Larry go" and rise again to the defense of her husband at the end. It is Larry living not Larry dead that she clings to, and she does this because to admit his death would make both life and love more difficult. Moreover, as is generally true of Miller's important women, Kate's final loyalty is to her husband; to him as a living, substantial being, she, like Linda in *Death of a Salesman,* has made an irrevocable commitment in love and sympathy which no knowledge *about* him can destroy.

FAMILY SHADOWS

Chris, on the other hand, is incapable of any such surrender of the letter of morality in the name of love or mercy; he cannot, as his father would have him, "see it human." At the rise of the curtain in Act II, Chris is seen dragging away the remains of Larry's memorial tree. The action is clearly symbolic; Chris, because of his own needs, has determined to free the family of the shadow of self-deception and guilt cast over it by the memory of Larry, to let in the light of truth. Yet, when the light comes, he is less able to bear it than the others. Ann, in the hope of love and marriage, rejects the seeds of hatred and remorse which her brother, George, offers her, and Kate sacrifices the dead son to the living father. But Chris has too much at stake; his life must vindicate the deaths of those who died in the war, which means that he must maintain an ideal image of himself or else be overwhelmed by his own sense of guilt. Because he is closely identified with his father, his necessary sense of personal dignity and worthiness depends upon his belief in the ideal image of his father; consequently, he can only accept the father's exposure as a personal defeat.

It becomes clear in the exchange between Chris and George Deever (Act II) that Chris has suspected his father but has suppressed his suspicions because he could not face the consequences—the condemnation of the father, whom he loves, and the condemnation of himself as polluted by sharing in the illicit spoils of war. Yet, this is precisely what the exposure of Joe Keller forces upon him, and Joe's arguments in self-defense—that he had expected the defective parts to be rejected, that what he did was done for the family, that business is business and none of it is "clean"—all shatter upon the hard shell of Chris's idealism not simply because they are, in fact, evasions and irrelevant half-truths, but because they cannot satisfy Chris's conscience. Consequently, even after Larry's suicide letter has finally brought to Joe a realization of his personal responsibility, Chris must go on to insist upon a public act of penance. The father becomes, indeed, a kind of scapegoat for the son; that is, if Joe expiates his crimes through the acceptance of a just punishment, then Chris will be relieved of his own burden of paralyzing guilt. His love of his father and his complicity with his father will then no longer imply his own unworthiness. In insisting that Joe must go to prison, Chris is, in effect, asking Joe to give him back his self-respect, so that he may be free to marry Ann and assume the life which is rightfully his. But Chris's inability to accept his father "as a man" leads Joe to believe that not only have his defenses crumbled but that the whole basis of his life is gone, and he kills himself.

A DUAL IMPRESSION

Because it forces upon the reader an awareness of the intricacies of human motivation and of human relationships, *All My Sons* leaves a dual impression: the action affirms the theme of the individual's responsibility to humanity, but, at the same time, it suggests that the standpoint of even so fine an ideal is not an altogether adequate one from which to evaluate human beings, and that a rigid idealism operating in the actual world of men entails suffering and waste, especially when the idealist is hagridden by his own ideals. There is no simple opposition here between those "who know" and those who "must learn," between those who possess the truth and those who have failed to grasp it, between the spiritually well and the spiritually sick. Moreover, the corruption and destruction of a man like Joe Keller, who is struggling to preserve what he conceives to be a just evaluation of himself in the eyes of his son, implies, in the context of the play, a deficiency not only in Keller's character but in the social environment in which he exists. Keller's appeal to the general ethics of the business community—

> If my money's dirty there ain't a clean nickel in the United
> States. Who worked for nothin' in that war? . . . Did they ship
> a gun or a truck outa Detroit before they got their price? . . .
> It's dollars and cents, nickels and dimes; war and peace, it's
> nickels and dimes, what's clean?

—is irrelevant to his personal defense; yet, it is an indictment of that community nonetheless. For it indicates that the
business community failed to provide any substantial values
which might have supplemented and counter-balanced
Keller's own limited, family-based ethics. From the business
community came only the impulse to which Chris also responds when he feels prompted to express his love for Ann
by saying, "I'm going to make a fortune for you!"

Furthermore, there is a sense in which Kate's words, "We
were all struck by the same lightning," are true; the lightning was the experience of the second World War—a mas-
sive social action in which they were all, willy-nilly, involved. It was the war that made it possible for some to profit
by the suffering and death of others and that created the special occasion of Joe Keller's temptation, which led in turn to
his son Larry's suicide and his wife's morbid obsession.
Chris Keller and George Deever brought something positive
out of the war—an ideal of brotherhood and a firmer, more
broadly based ethic—but George, as he appears in the play,
is paying in remorse for the principles that led him to reject
his father, and Chris's idealism is poisoned at the source by
shame and guilt, which are also products of his war experience and which make it impossible for him to temper justice
with mercy either for himself or anyone else.

CHAPTER 3

Staging and Structure

READINGS ON
ALL MY SONS

An Intricately Structured Play

June Schlueter

Although *All My Sons'* plot works by coincidence and contrivance, June Schlueter argues that the emotional power that emerges out of the play's action easily overcomes any apparent heavy-handedness. In *All My Sons*, Miller mastered the difficult art of bringing the past into the play's present, which is particularly important for a play that explores the consequences of past actions. By deftly infusing jarring moments and subtle forebodings into a comfortable, ostensibly "normal" domestic environment, Miller gradually quickens the play's pace and increases its pressures on the characters until the moment of crisis inevitably arrives. In the manner of a Shakespearean tragedy, truth and order—and the hope of redemption—are finally restored. Schlueter is a professor of English at Lafayette College, Pennsylvania.

All My Sons opened at Broadway's Coronet Theater on January 29, 1947, in a production directed by Elia Kazan and starring Ed Begley, Beth Merrill, and Arthur Kennedy. It played to an audience that, four years earlier, read the news account of the Truman Committee's investigation into allegedly faulty airplane parts manufactured in Ohio and that was particularly responsive to the question of wartime responsibility, only recently having participated in its country's "return to normalcy." Not surprisingly, the play was an immediate success, running for some 347 performances, winning the New York Drama Critics' Circle Award, and establishing the thirty-two-year-old Miller as among the most promising of America's playwrights. . . .

Excerpted from *Arthur Miller* (New York: Ungar, 1987) by June Schlueter. Copyright © 1987 by the Ungar Publishing Co. Reprinted with permission from June Schlueter.

ALL MY SONS' DRAMATIC CONVENTIONS

All My Sons relies on coincidence and contrivance. The play works in production, when an audience is more likely to excuse heavy-handedness and yield to the drama's emotional power. But as text, it cannot cover its seams, and a reader may well be disturbed by Kate's casual remark that her husband hasn't been sick in fifteen years—which leads to the discovery of his lie; by Annie's long-concealed letter from Larry, which clears up the doubt concerning his disappearance; and by Keller's sudden remorse and suicide.

Despite these remnants of nineteenth-century conventions, however, and their seeming incompatibility with the twentieth-century realistic play, Miller crafts his drama deftly, drawing for its structure on the retrospective technique that has come to be identified as "Ibsenesque." In such a structure, the past continually intrudes upon the present, and the exposition often sustains itself through the final act, when the critical piece of information necessary for the play's dramatic ending is revealed. Miller found such a structure particularly hospitable for this story, which insists on the consequences of past action. As Miller notes in the introduction to *Collected Plays,* the question was not whether Keller or Chris could ameliorate the consequences of the crime: "The stakes remaining are purely the conscience of Joe Keller and its awakening to the evil he has done, and the conscience of his son in the face of what he has discovered about his father. . . . The structure of the play is designed to bring a man into the direct path of the consequences he has wrought."

Throughout *All My Sons,* Miller works gradually at bringing the audience's level of awareness to that of those in the drama: Keller knows he is responsible for the pilots' deaths; he knows why his wife must continue to believe her son is alive; and he knows that his neighbors know of his guilt. Similarly, Keller's wife, Kate, shares this knowledge. On the other hand, Chris, whose level of awareness coincides with that of the audience, has believed in his father's innocence and tries in earnest to persuade his mother to accept Larry's death. Annie, who returns to the Keller household after several years' absence, has adjusted to the death of her sweetheart, Larry, and is now ready to turn her affections to Chris. She, it turns out, possesses the critical piece of information about Larry's death, which places her above all the other characters in one respect, but, until the play is well under way and her brother George appears, she does not know that her father is serving the prison sentence that is rightfully Keller's. As the play proceeds, providing information to Annie and Chris and, with respect to Larry's death, to Joe and Kate, the audience adjusts its perspectives to accommodate the new evidence, becoming increasingly suspicious of Keller's integrity. With Chris and Annie, it discovers Keller's guilt, and, with Joe and Kate, it learns that Keller's action was responsible for the death of his own son as well.

THE USE OF TIME IN THE FIRST ACT

All My Sons takes place in late August, three and one-half years after the loss of the twenty-one pilots and the report that Larry was missing in action. Within twenty-four hours of play time, the Kellers' lives move from tranquillity to calamity, from ignorance or denial of the truth to discovery or admission. The action takes place in the Kellers' backyard, a typically American setting with trees and lawn and a sheltered cove in which Keller relaxes with the Sunday paper. Neighbors on both sides—Jim and Sue Bayliss and Frank and Lydia Lubey—feel free to stop by to share the paper or to chat, lending assurance of the perfectly normal routine of this family's comfortable life.

But act 1 gradually prepares its characters for the catastrophe that will follow, teasing its audience with sour notes that intrude upon this atmosphere of normality. When Frank stops by, he notices what an audience would also have noticed immediately: the slender apple tree downstage left lies toppled, a casualty of the previous night's storm. Keller and son worry about how Kate will respond to the destruction of the tree the family planted in tribute to Larry. As it turns out, Kate already knows about the tree, having witnessed its fate at four A.M., when a vision of Larry flying high above the house in his plane urged her outside. Kate becomes an important figure in the opening act, creating interest through her stolid refusal to accept Larry's death and her repeated insistence that he may yet return. At her request, Frank has been working on Larry's horoscope, which, if it shows that the fatal day in November was a "favorable" day for Larry, will reinforce her hope. Kate's obsession only deepens when Larry's old girlfriend, Annie, returns for a visit at Chris's invitation; she strenuously opposes an alliance between her second son and the woman she still perceives as "Larry's girl."

The effect of such early interest in Kate and in the developing conflict between her and her son Chris over Annie is to delay the interest the play will gradually but forcefully develop in Keller, who will prove to be the central character—one of the first in a line of strong-willed, self-deluded men who typify Miller's vision of the American family. Such a masculine figurehead is both its backbone and its bane. But there are hints in act 1 that Joe will be at the center of the drama. Bert, one of the neighborhood boys, rushes into the Keller yard speaking of law breakers and law enforcers and begging to see the prison in the Keller basement. Keller knows the terms of the game he has encouraged in the neighborhood, but he laughingly sends the boy off without showing him the jail. Speaking delightedly about this game to his wife, Keller explains that the kids took an interest in him when he returned from the penitentiary, but then they began confusing the former inmate with the detective. Kate is quick to correct Keller, suggesting it was not *they* who got confused. The game her husband plays has much to do with his own history, which naturally becomes part of the discussion with the long-absent Annie. Deever, whom Annie and her brother have disowned and whom Keller calls a "little man," is in jail, the consequence of Keller's deliberate confusion of the facts. The criminal became the law enforcer, misrepresented the facts, and assumed the role of the innocent. Upon his return from jail following his exoneration, Keller got out of his car at the corner so he could walk the distance of the block, his head held defiantly high against the neighbors' scorn. But since then, poker games and neighborly rapport have been restored, and the criminal has become the pillar of society.

Similarly, Chris speaks of his days in the army, where he led a corps of men who displayed uncommon friendship and loyalty, defending their colleagues even at the expense of their own lives. Because he escaped the fate of so many of them, Chris feels a vague sense of guilt over his own survival. Though too early in the play to make the connection explicitly, this introspective moment offers a contrast to the guilt-free Keller, who has unconscionably let Deever take the blame. And then Kate responds twice with a disturbing anger, an insistence so impassioned as to be suspicious. She reprimands the child for believing there is a basement jail, then returns to Keller's curious question, the central question of the play, "What have I got to hide?" And when Kate defends her belief in Larry's survival, she reminds her husband, with uncommon intensity, that he above all has got to believe.

By the end of act 1, the audience is sure the play will be Keller's and is anxious about the turn of events. Annie's brother, George, having traveled seven hundred miles from New York to Columbus to tell his father of Annie's impending marriage, telephones. He is coming to the Kellers' home, apparently with some new and disturbing knowledge. Alone on stage, Kate and Keller react. Kate fears George's arrival and cautions her husband to be smart. Keller is angry, arrogant, and self-assured. The call redirects attention to the case of the cracked cylinders and to the question of what Keller has to hide.

A STORY OF FIDELITY AND BELIEF

Miller's second act offers an effective balance of bitterness and sweetness, of anxiety and relief, prolonging its two dramatic questions: How will Annie react to George's belief in his father's innocence—will she still marry into the family that is "covered with blood"—and how will Keller react— will he admit he framed his partner? Was he, in fact, responsible for the shipment of the cylinders? The act takes place later that day, at twilight. Chris is sawing off the broken apple tree and suggesting to his mother that without it there is more light. The atmosphere is one of anticipation: they are waiting for the arrival of George, whom Jim has gone to fetch at the station. Chris, assured in his belief that the family has nothing to hide, seems unconcerned, but Kate is overreacting, pleading with Chris to protect them. She fears the case will be reopened and that Deever's story—that Keller made him do it—will prevail. Near hysteria, she begs Chris to help them—and to send Annie home, for she is of the Deever clan, which hates them. Keller, by contrast, is not worrying, or at least he is expressing his concern more passively—through sleeping.

In the moments before George's arrival, though, even as Keller sleeps, the father-son conflict so familiar to readers of Miller begins to take form. Annie has a chance conversation with neighbor Sue about Chris, which is especially revealing. She dislikes Chris for his idealism and proceeds to impute a fundamental dishonesty to him since he, despite his "holiness," still works in his father's business. Clearly, the neighbors have never believed in Keller's innocence and now resent not only his freedom at the expense of Deever but Chris's acceptance of the tainted firm as the source of his livelihood, even as he silently preaches perfection.

Annie, upset, immediately confronts Chris with Sue's opinions, which Chris dismisses as just that. Chris, after all, is attached to his parents, and his love for his father is particularly—and reciprocally—intense. Keller, in fact, has worked all his life for his sons, and, with Larry gone, his hopes rest completely in Chris. Earlier in the play, when Chris appealed to Keller to side with him in his desire to marry Annie, he threatened to leave the business if Keller did not support his cause, and the astonished father capitulated. Keller's need to leave his life's effort as a legacy to his son anticipates a similarly intense—and misdirected—desire in Miller's later central character [in *Death of a Salesman*], Willy Loman. As with the deluded salesman, Keller must have his son be heir or see the commitment of his life invalidated. With Willy, a dream is at stake, but with Keller, Chris's participation in the family business is all that keeps the older man from being a murderer. When, later in the play, Keller confesses his treachery, he justifies it in terms of the prospect of losing his life's work, of robbing himself of the legacy he has promised his sons. He shipped out the risky cylinder heads so he could buy time to prove his business viable and to preserve the business for Chris. Yet Keller still calls the firm J.O. Keller, not J.O. Keller & Son; despite Chris's commitment to the firm, his name has not yet been attached to it. George makes a point of this a bit later, understanding that, though Chris may defend his father as head of the "Holy Family," what is at least an unconscious doubt has prevented him from becoming a partner. Chris can barely assimilate his father's later plea: "I did it for you."

Just before George's arrival, then, a gossipy neighbor has set up the father-son relationship that is central to a play that is, finally, a story of fidelity and belief. Bert believes there is a prison under the Keller house, despite Kate's testimony to the contrary. Yet Kate holds a more dangerous, adult delusion: that her husband is innocent, her son Larry alive. In the first instance, she knows that belief in Keller's innocence necessitates a lie, and she has, for over three years, pretended to others what she has never been able to pretend to herself. But believing in Larry's survival is a bit more manageable, for she has no proof to the contrary. Over the years, though, Kate has connected the events so inextricably that her profession of faith in Larry has become a surrogate expression of faith in her husband. Like Keller, she serves the image of the American family as sacrosanct; neither is willing to admit that their Holy Family is headed by a moral weakling, a man whose culpability is compounded by his refusal to admit his wrong. Neither Keller nor Kate is so self-deluded as to believe their own protestations of innocence, but their belief in the sanctity of the Keller family motivates their perpetuation of the lie. Chris is heir to his parents' principles and morality, yet, being an honest man and an idealist, he can believe only in the purity of his father's behavior. His is the more treacherous kind of self-delusion, for Chris believes religiously in the lie. He never suspected his father's guilt because he could not accommodate that guilt with his vision of self or of family. With his parents, he has joined in the lie—though clearly without any awareness that he is doing so. The neighbors, by contrast, are aware of Keller's guilt, of Kate's cover-up, and of Chris's ignorance by design; they admire Keller's cunning but detest his morality. Yet still, in deference to some abstract concept of neighborliness, they chat with the Kellers and even pretend to trust Joe at cards. Only Annie and George seem to accept the loss of faith attendant upon their father's conviction. They assume the law is right and disown their father as a moral weakling who has committed an unconscionable crime.

THE KELLERS SNAP UNDER THE PRESSURE OF TRUTH

The play is a web, then, of homespun fidelities, of faith placed and misplaced, a network of belief that, like the apple tree, snaps under pressure. And the arrival of George begins the weakening of several of the strands, for it prompts Sue to speak contemptuously to Annie of Chris's "phoney idealism," and it reveals the restoration of George's belief in his father.

Deever, of course, has been the victim of the Keller family's deception, and now George has just returned from telling his father that Annie is about to marry into that family. George is himself a lawyer, a man who should see clearly the difference between right and wrong but who has himself been duped for years, too ready to accept Joe's story over his father's. Tellingly, he enters the Keller household wearing his father's hat—and he has come to take Annie home. This time, George believes his father's story. After three and a half years, he now sees his father as Keller's victim and refuses to allow the moral taint of the Keller family to claim his sister. But, even here, Miller does things gradually: though vehement and bitter when he enters, George falls prey to nostalgia, to Kate's charm, and to the weaknesses he knows his father possesses. Joe's tactic is to welcome George with warmth, arranging a meeting with Lydia, his former girlfriend; to discredit Deever by cataloging other moments of his weakness; and to extend himself generously, offering Deever a position with the firm when in a year or two he gets out of jail. Kate works at George's sense of nostalgia; the two were always friends, and she has remembered to provide him with his favorite grape juice.

The seduction is too much for George, and the bitter reunion turns into a sweet one, with talk of childhood experiences and preparations for the evening meal. Relaxed and appeased, George confesses he never felt at home anywhere but there. He compliments Kate on her youthful appearance and tells Joe he is "amazingly the same." Keller responds by saying he has no time to get sick, and then Kate, endorsing her husband's pride in his good health, speaks the fatal line: "He hasn't been laid up in fifteen years," breaking the spell. Despite Joe's immediate qualification—"Except my flu during the war"—George is alert and challenging, for it was Keller's alleged illness that kept him from the plant on the day the cracked cylinder heads came off the line. Ironically, at the moment when the Kellers are threatened so darkly and so inescapably, at the moment when Kate's worst fears are about to be realized, Miller brings Frank onstage with the announcement that he has completed Larry's horoscope: November 25 was a "favorable" day; Larry must be alive.

But Larry is about to die, for Kate's belief in him need not be sustained beyond the revelation of her husband's guilt, which George's anger now presages. Kate and George both want Annie to leave, but Chris reacts with passion, prohibiting further mention of Larry and directing George to leave. Annie joins Chris in telling her brother to go.

In the quarrel between Kate and Chris that ensues, Kate finally reveals the truth:

> MOTHER: Your brother's alive, darling, because if he's dead,
> your father killed him. Do you understand me now? As long

as you live, that boy is alive. God does not let a son be killed by his father. Now you see, don't you? Now you see.

Defeated, Keller pleads that his son never flew a P-40, then justifies his decision: forty years of his life were at risk the day he ordered the cylinders shipped; he took the chance for Chris's sake. But Chris's sense of moral responsibility, unlike his father's, extends beyond the personal, beyond the family to the larger family of which he felt a part during the war.

A RESTITUTION OF THE SOCIAL ORDER

Father and son collide over an issue that will resonate through Miller's plays: the conflict between the social and the personal. In this play, as in others that Miller will later write, a man's personal integrity, even his survival, depends on his denial of his social responsibility. Had Keller not wanted so desperately to pass on the family business to his son, he might not have been so profit-oriented as a businessman. He might have halted production of the cylinders and not met the government contract, despite the financial consequence. But, yielding to individual and family pride, he risked processing the faulty parts and lost the bet. Then, faced again with a moral crisis—whether to confess his complicity or look to Deever as a scapegoat—he chose the latter, necessitating a life of deception afterwards. Once Chris understands what his father has done, once he has identified the heinous consequences of Keller's having placed the personal above the social, the final act moves inexorably toward restitution of the social order through the offender's death. Keller leaves in his wake the broken relationship between Annie and Chris, a dead son, and a family fallen like the apple tree; the sense of a moral and social order prevails.

Keller's guilt established, the dramatic question shifts from "What does Joe Keller have to hide?" to "What will happen now that everyone knows?" Act 2, like act 1, ends with a heavy curtain, Chris pounding his fist on his father's shoulder and weeping, not knowing what to do.

Several hours pass during the interlude between acts, bringing the play's action to two A.M. the following day. Act 3 opens with the contemplative Kate rocking on the porch chair, in moonlight. She is waiting for Chris to return. Jim talks with her as she rocks, revealing that the neighbors always knew, and assuring her that Chris will come back. While they wait, the elder Kellers try to salvage what is left of their lives, Joe turning meekly to Kate for guidance and she counseling yet another lie: if he told Chris he was willing to go to prison, Chris surely would not ask him to go, but perhaps he would forgive him. Even now, Keller cannot accept responsibility, self-righteously asking what there was that Chris needed to forgive. Acknowledging Kate as the accomplice that she undoubtedly has been, he characteristically shifts the blame once again, faulting her for wanting money. Kate sees that her husband is trying to exonerate himself on familial grounds: "Joe, Joe . . . it don't excuse it that you did it for the family," but Keller insists, "It's got to excuse it!"

The moment is more critical for Keller than the revelation of his guilt in the earlier act. As Miller notes in the introduction to *Collected Plays,*

> Joe Keller's trouble, in a word, is not that he cannot tell right from wrong but that his cast of mind cannot admit that he, personally, has any viable connection with his world, his universe, or his society. He is not a partner in society, but an incorporated member, so to speak, and you cannot sue personally the officers of a corporation.

Keller has always believed in the family as an autonomous entity and the highest principle:

> Nothin's bigger than that. . . . I'm his father and he's my son, and if there's something bigger than that I'll put a bullet in my head!

Within the hour, Keller does put a bullet in his head, in a gesture that both insists on his own belief in family and tentatively acknowledges that his sons, Chris and Larry, may be right in seeing something bigger. Unwilling to relinquish his belief, Keller argues with Chris when he returns, defending himself as a man no worse than others. Ironically, Chris never measured him against other men, never even saw him as a man but only as his father, and until the revelation of act 2, Chris's vision of Keller coincided with his abstract ideal. His philosophy of family affirmed his father's, but now Chris understands what he had known in his army days and had ignored—intentionally or unintentionally—since the court case: that there is something bigger than the family. It is a belief endorsed by brother Larry, through the letter he wrote to Annie on the day of his suicide, which Chris now reads aloud. Larry could not live with the shame of his father's involvement in the deaths of his fellow men. Keller understands that to Larry, "they were all my sons. And I guess they were, I guess they were."

THE HOPE OF REDEMPTION

In "The Family in Modern Drama," Miller avers that all great plays deal with a single problem:

> How may a man make of the outside world a home? How and in what ways must he struggle, what must he strive to change and overcome within himself and outside himself if he is to find the safety, the surroundings of love, the ease of soul, the sense of identity and honor which, evidently, all men have connected in their memories with the idea of family?

By the time Keller has the capacity to acknowledge his membership in a larger, social family, whose principles, when in conflict with those of the private family, must prevail, he has already so violated its moral assumptions that even a prison sentence will not absolve him. To Miller, Keller threatens society not because he has sold faulty parts to the military but because that crime has "roots in a certain relationship of the individual to society, and to a certain indoctrination he embodies, which, if dominant, can mean a jungle existence for all of us no matter how high our buildings soar."

If there is hope for redemption among the remaining Kellers at play's end, that hope rests in Chris, who ends the act sobbing at Kate's feet as she frees him to live. Chris will leave the Keller household, he will not marry Annie, and he will renew the lesson of his army days that his father—and Willy Loman after him—had such a difficult time learning. For Miller, the struggle between father and son "for recognition and forgiveness," in both *All My Sons* and *Death of a Salesman,* is insufficient: "But when it extends itself out of the family circle and into society, it broaches those questions of social status, social honor and recognition, which expand its vision and lift it out of the merely particular toward the fate of the generality of men."

A Taut Mystery That Operates at Three Levels of Significance

Neil Carson

The unspoken tensions that lie beneath the placid surface of the Kellers' suburban life, the sudden flood of revelations, and the host of tragic conse- quences that follow make *All My Sons* seem like a tightly constructed mystery. Yet, Neil Carson also notes what he calls three levels of significance in *All My Sons*: the cosmic, the social, and the psychologi- cal. Kate Keller's belief in astrology, Chris and Joe Keller's conflicting views regarding what responsi- bility is, and the psychology of lost faith that tor- ments both Chris and Joe at the end of the play give *All My Sons* a remarkable sense of balance. Neil Carson is a professor of English at the University of Guelph, Canada.

[*All My Sons*] originated . . . in a true incident told to [Miller] by a friend. This story concerned a family from the Middle West which had been destroyed when the daughter had re- ported her father to the authorities for selling faulty machin- ery to the Army. Miller says that he visualised the second-act climax to *All My Sons* almost before the narrator had fin- ished the story. Nevertheless, the actual writing of the work took some two years. In the final version the manufacturer, Joe Keller, has not only shipped out defective airplane parts, but he has also escaped the consequences of his actions by pinning the blame on his partner. Seemingly undisturbed by the death of twenty-one flyers who crashed in planes with his cracked cylinder-heads, Joe Keller has returned to his home, regained the affection of his neighbours, rebuilt his business and generally resumed his successful life. His el- dest son, Chris, on his return from war joined the family

Excerpted from *Arthur Miller*, by Neil Carson. Copyright © 1982 by Neil Carson. Reprinted with permission from Palgrave Publishers Ltd.

firm convinced that his father was innocent of the crime for which he was tried and acquitted. Meanwhile, Keller's partner, Steve Deever, who was convicted and is serving a prison sentence has been abandoned by both his children, Ann and George, who have not believed his protestations of innocence. The Deever family has moved from the neighbourhood to avoid the scandal, but Chris has been writing to Ann. Ann had been engaged to the younger Keller son, Larry, who was reported missing in the war and has never been found. The play opens with Ann coming to visit the Kellers on Chris's invitation.

A TAUT MYSTERY STORY

The drama unfolds like a tautly written mystery story. The apparently placid surface of the Keller family life is disturbed first by the arrival of Ann and then by the announcement that George will also be coming to visit. The first act ends with an ominous tension between Joe Keller and his wife, Kate, and with her cryptic warning to him to 'be smart'. The second act reopens the latent conflict between the two families. George has become convinced that his father has been framed by Joe, and he is determined that Ann will not marry Chris. Ann remains sceptical of these new charges, and even George is in danger of being charmed by the Kellers until Kate lets it slip that Joe was not sick, as he had maintained at the trial, on the day the cylinder heads had been delivered. Unable to persuade Ann to go with him, George leaves. In a quarrel with his mother, Chris finally learns the truth, and when he confronts his father, Joe admits that he did give the order to ship out the defective parts.

The third act brings a further revelation in the form of a letter which Ann had received from Larry just before he had been reported missing. In it he confessed that he had been shattered by the news of his father's arrest and was intending to commit suicide. This news destroys Kate's obsessive belief that Larry is still alive and finally overcomes her opposition to a marriage between Chris and Ann. It also brings home to Joe the full loathsomeness of his antisocial act by making him see that the death of his own son is a direct consequence of his actions. Joe agrees to turn himself in to the district attorney, but instead he goes upstairs and shoots himself.

All My Sons is greatly indebted to the work of Henrik Ibsen, who adapted methods of Greek tragedy to realist drama. Ibsen perfected what has been called 'the play of ripe circumstance' in which, in the course of a relatively short period of stage time, the events of a whole lifetime are put into a perspective which gives tragic significance to the catastrophe. Miller has obviously learned from the Norwegian master how to withhold information about the past until it is most useful dramatically, and how to create a sense of an inexorable web of cause and effect. But *All My Sons* is more than a slavish imitation. The principal difference is in the attitudes of the two dramatists. Whereas Ibsen is primarily concerned with the consequences of past action (the birds coming home to roost), Miller is more interested in the reaction which follows understanding. In Miller, the moment of awareness is always preparation for a moment of choice.

THREE LEVELS OF SIGNIFICANCE

All My Sons can be thought of as operating on three levels of significance: the cosmic, the social and the psychological. Originally, the dramatist gave far more emphasis to Kate's astrological beliefs, but in the course of revision this element of the play was reduced. . . . She comes to realise that her faith in astrology is an illusion. Convinced at the opening of the play that 'God does not let a son be killed by his father,' she comes to see that she had been deliberately blinding herself to what she did not want to admit. But Kate's story in the final version of the play is subordinated to those of Joe and Chris, and the major focus appears to be on the conflict between two kinds of social code.

It is this stratum of the play which seems most old-fashioned and didactic. The conflict embodied here is between two sets of values—the one represented by Kate and Joe Keller, the other embodied in different ways in the younger generation of Chris, Ann, George and Larry. The Kellers epitomise the capitalistic system of competition, the 'land of the great big dogs, [where] you don't love a man . . . you eat him'. George and Ann speak for a world of justice . . . where everyone gets what he deserves. Chris and Larry articulate a still higher ideal, a New Testament law of love and co-operation rather than the Mosaic 'eye for an eye'. For Chris, this ideal is a product of his experience during the war when he saw men who 'killed themselves for each other'. In the destruction and horror of combat, Chris believed, 'one new thing was made. A kind of—responsibility. Man for man', which gave life meaning. Chris's restlessness and moral urgency derive from his sense that that meaning has been lost in civilian life, and that the men who fought and died have been betrayed by those who never understood what the fighting had been about.

The conflict between the generations is complicated, however, by the Kellers' curious incomprehension of the issues. Both Kate and Joe justify what has happened on the ground that it was done with the very best motive—love for their children. Whatever unfortunate consequences Joe's actions may have had on individuals outside the family are rationalised away as inevitable results of the system, or of the 'way the world is'. As Miller says of Joe, he thinks of himself, not as a 'partner in society, but as an incorporated member' who cannot be sued for the wrong doing of the corporation.

The design of *All My Sons*, therefore, is the confrontation of a man with all of the consequences of his actions. It proceeds in two phases. The play is not, like [Greek tragedian Sophocles'] *Oedipus*, the uncovering of an unknown sin so horrible in its author's eyes that he blinds himself; nor is it, like [Shakespeare's] *Hamlet*, the attempt to unmask a criminal anxious to keep his guilt secret. The simple exposing of his unashamed involvement does not bring Keller any new insight into himself or his actions. When Chris confronts him with his deed, Keller continues to excuse himself. In order to bring the play to a conclusion, Joe must see and admit his guilt. This second climax is brought about by Ann. Armed with her letter from Larry, she makes Kate and then Joe give up their delusions about being untouched by the consequences of Joe's actions. Only when tragedy touches him directly does Keller seem able to sympathise with the suffering of others and recognise his connection with the rest of humanity. Even at the end, however, Joe remains evasive. Unable to face trial and imprisonment, he kills himself.

Judging from the title of the play, it is this conflict of social values with which the dramatist is primarily concerned. But there is a deeper, psychological significance in *All My Sons* which is examined less thoroughly. This involves the question of faith, and is closely related to issues raised in [Miller's first Broadway play] *The Man Who Had All the Luck*. Kate's loss of belief has been mentioned, but Miller does not show us in detail how she responds to this disillusionment. In the case of Joe Keller, however, and still more in that of his son, the playwright is interested in exploring the psychological reaction to a loss of faith. Joe Keller has based his life on the conviction that nothing is bigger than the relationship between a father and a son. When he comes to realise that his responsibility is not restricted to his family but extends to a universe of people beyond the property line, he cannot face his own past. His suicide is partly an act of penance for his previous deeds, but it is also the act of a man who cannot live with himself.

Chris, too, is disillusioned in the play when he discovers that his father whom he had idolised is no better than other men. The pain caused by that insight is intense and has the effect of temporarily paralysing his will—'I never saw you as a man. I saw you as my father. I can't look at you this way. I can't look at myself.' As a result of his sorrow, Chris vacillates between an inability to face his father and an over-zealous vindictiveness. When he hears the shot, he is overcome by doubt and remorse, and it is Kate who encourages him to take control of his life—'Don't take it on yourself. Forget now. Live.'

All My Sons Was Deeply Influenced by Sophocles and Ibsen

Robert Hogan

All My Sons is structured around the eventual revelation of a crime committed years before the action begins; therefore, it belongs to a dramatic subgenre mastered by the Greek tragedian Sophocles and the great Norwegian realist Henrik Ibsen. Robert Hogan maintains that Arthur Miller skillfully fuses explanations of what happened in the past to the play's present action, thereby allowing the consequences of the past to be revealed. Though *All My Sons* lacks the lyrical beauty of Sophocles' *Oedipus Rex* and the irony of Ibsen's best work, its austere style and flawless structure ensure its success. Hogan taught English at the University of California, Davis, and published many works on Irish and American drama.

Miller's first really accomplished work was the play *All My Sons*, which was produced on January 29, 1947, and had a Broadway run of 347 performances. The play established Miller as a dramatist of much promise and was given the Drama Critics' Circle Award as the best American play of the season. That award was something of an overestimation, for the same season saw the first production of O'Neill's[1] masterly *The Iceman Cometh.* Nevertheless, *All My Sons* is a strong, traditional, well-made play whose technique insists upon comparison with the realistic plays of Ibsen.[2] Like them, *All My Sons* begins almost immediately before the climax of its story. Most of the story has occurred before the curtain rises and is revealed by exposition subtly interwoven

1. American dramatist Eugene O'Neill (1888–1953)   2. Norwegian dramatist Henrik Ibsen (1828–1906)

Excerpted from *Arthur Miller: University of Minnesota Pamphlets on American Writers*, no. 40, by Robert Hogan, 1964. Reprinted with permission from the University of Minnesota Press.

with the current action. Actually, this structure was not
unique with Miller or Ibsen or even Racine.[3] One may find
precisely the same structure in *Oedipus Rex;*[4] in Sophocles'
play, as in Miller's, the revelation of a criminal whose crime
has occurred years earlier is the crux of the present action.
However, in Miller's play the Oedipus character is split in
two—one half being the father and criminal and the other
half the son and detective.

ALL MY SONS HAS MANY PLOTS AND COUNTERPLOTS

This structure is difficult to handle, for the playwright must
explain rather than dramatize most of the action, and the
great bulk of exposition always threatens to dissipate the
dramatic impact of the play. There are probably three chief

---

3. French dramatist Jean-Baptiste Racine (1639–1699)   4. Greek tragedian Sophocles
(496 B.C.–406 B.C.) is best known for his play *Oedipus Rex.*

A SUBURBAN GRAVEYARD

In 1947, just as All My Sons *was about to open on Broadway, Arthur Miller was mystified by the presence of a low
hump in the middle of the stage, which the actors had some difficulty stepping over. Confronting the stage manager about this
hump, Miller found out the extent to which a play's stage props
can enhance its emotional atmosphere.*

When the set was first brought in, I was puzzled by a low
hump in the middle of the grassy backyard, around which the
actors were forced to make their way lest they trip. The women
were especially inconvenienced because their heels caught on
it, and I asked [director Elia] Kazan why it was there. Suppressing a persecuted grin, he quietly confided, "It's a grave."

"A grave! This is their backyard!"

"But the set signifies a graveyard. I'm not sure, maybe Max is
right. Why don't you ask him to explain it, and tell me what he
says."

Mordecai Gorelik, known as Max, was another Group veteran, a choleric genius who designed sets that might seem to
be a dentist's office or a gym or whatever but were organized,
at least in his mind, around a metaphoric statement condens-
ing the central image of the play at hand. I went to Max with
the worry that the actors were going to fall over his hump and
destroy my play. He was a beardless Abraham, a ramrod-
straight fanatic with the self-certainty of a terrorist and the

ways to combat this threat: by the evocative beauty of the dialogue, by irony, and by an adroit blending of current action with explanation of past action. In his *Oedipus Rex*, Sophocles superbly managed all three ways. In his social plays, Ibsen lacked poetry, but his permeating irony largely compensated for the realistic flatness of his style, and he did blend his past and present action with incomparable adroitness. In *All My Sons*, Miller handles his plot consummately, but he notably lacks both the poetry and the irony. Nevertheless, structure alone can carry a play very far, and Miller's play, because of its structure, remains absorbing theater.

It is the story of Joe Keller, a small manufacturer, who during the war allowed some faulty engine blocks to be shipped to the air force. When a number of planes crashed, Keller and his partner were brought to trial. Keller was finally released and his partner blamed, although Keller him-

---

smile—when he demolished an opponent in argument it just managed to flicker over his mouth—of a blood-covered avenging angel.

"Tripping? I didn't see anybody tripping."

"Well, they have slightly, and it makes them uncertain."

"Talk to the director if they're uncertain, uncertainty is his job."

"But what is the point of it, Max—a rise like that in the middle of the stage?"

"You have written a graveyard play," he said as categorically as if he were reading each word in lights behind my eyes, "and not some factual report. The play is taking place in a cemetery where their son is buried, and he is also their buried conscience reaching up to them out of the earth. Even if it inconveniences them it will keep reminding them what the hell all this acting is really *about*. The bump stays!" In fact, I gradually had to admit that in some indefinable way the mound did seem to unify the performances around a single subliminal preoccupation that had a certain power. And if one of them tripped on it occasionally, perhaps it did serve to remind them that the play was indeed about a bad conscience. But whether it worked or was meaningless, Max terrorized Kazan and me and everyone else into believing that it did, the alternative being to confront him, a suicidal act.

Excerpted from Arthur Miller, *Timebends: A Life*. New York: Grove Press, 1987, pp. 274–75.

self was really responsible. The theme, then, is one of morality and money, and the action centers around the attempt of Keller's son Chris to find the truth and to fix the responsibility, and of Keller to avoid his responsibility. The point of his guilt is only brought home to him after a letter is produced proving that his other son Larry had also considered his father guilty and had died in combat as a kind of expiation. Then Joe recognizes that the other pilots who died were "all my sons" and in expiation he kills himself.

This action does not at first dominate the play. It is brought to a head by the current action, a false plot which seems at the beginning to be the story's major substance. Chris has asked his brother's fiancée home because he intends to marry her. However, Chris's mother refuses to believe that Larry really died in battle, and much of the play's first two acts is an attempt to convince her, so that Chris and Ann may marry.

As in *Oedipus Rex* or [Ibsen's] *Ghosts,* the real plot emerges from the present action like a ghost from the past. It comes to dominate that action and to be the center of the play. This plot from the past, even in the beginning of the play, is constantly intruded; we are constantly reminded of Joe's trial and Larry's death. Such a technique may seem at first to slow the pace, until we see that it is revealing the real action. When such a parallel plot is well handled, there is a suspenseful tension as the relationship between past and present becomes ever clearer.

ALL MY SONS POSSESSES BOTH ECONOMY AND TRAGEDY

Like Ibsen's social plays, Miller's play is economical. All of his characters, even the minor ones, have an integral relation to the theme. No characters are introduced merely to illustrate or to facilitate the mechanics of the plot. Such economy emphasizes the play's closeness to traditional austere tragedy. This is a family tragedy; the father is a man of some importance who falls from power to ignominy. The lives of his entire family are blighted by his crime. Such a description might just as well apply to the royal family of [Oedipus'] Thebes or to the Alving family of Norway.

There is even in the play a hint of fate inexorably guiding the destinies of the characters. It is the ghost from the past, the dead son, whose words precipitate the tragic climax. In one of the minor characters who is preparing a horoscope of the dead son, the play even has a prophet. That last fact suggests the distance between the austere stylized tragedy of Sophocles and Racine and the austere realistic tragedy of Ibsen and Miller. Ibsen had attempted to inject the supernatural into some of his realistic dramas—such as, for instance, the white horses in *Rosmersholm*. Perhaps his intention was to compensate for a lack of grandeur and tragic import which might derive from realistic dialogue and a middleclass setting. Ibsen was not, however, entirely successful in bringing a sense of fate into the front parlor, and turned away in his last plays from the illusion of total realism. Miller's intrusion of the supernatural is even more apologetically introduced than Ibsen's white horses. Most of the characters discount the horoscope, and the audience takes Miller's prophet as a mildly comic relief in a basically serious play. Consequently, Miller loses even the small effect that Ibsen gained, and his play seems smaller.

That smallness is particularly evident in the play's conclusion. Toward the end of the last act, Miller increases the intensity of the action to an extent that seems overwrought and frenetic when compared to the ambling and realistic tone of the earlier part. There is in the theater, unless the play is done excellently, some incongruity, as if the ending of an Elizabethan blood tragedy had been attached to a play by [English dramatist] Terence Rattigan.

Nevertheless, despite its lack of irony, of really composed dialogue, and of characters who live outside of a theater, *All My Sons* is a real accomplishment. Its characters, if somewhat flat, do not have the dishonest flatness of many stage characters. Its theme seems likely to remain deeply pertinent for American society, and it is a model of structural craftsmanship. Probably its excellences of theme and structure will keep it fresh for as long as those excellences kept green the plays of [English dramatist] John Galsworthy. That is certainly a limited immortality, but scarcely a contemptible one.

Emotional Power Is Sacrificed for the Sake of Structural Integrity

Ronald Hayman

Through its artful use of symbols, an array of minor characters, and the strong connection Arthur Miller makes between the Kellers' private desires and the very public themes they represent, *All My Sons* is a remarkably well-structured play. Ronald Hayman pays homage to Miller's mastery of his craft, but nevertheless feels that the play's dense structure undermines the emotional power of the characters' inner changes. Therefore, in the most vital scenes, *All My Sons'* language cannot live up to the emotional tensions its structure has created and moved toward. A widely acknowledged expert on twentieth-century drama, Hayman has written *Brecht: A Biography* and *British Theatre Since 1955: A Reassessment.*

In performance, what is most immediately striking [about *All My Sons*] is the naturalness of the backyard life—the leisureliness of family life on a Sunday morning, the slightly strained camaraderie of the exchanges of weak wisecracks with the neighbours, the intra-family plotting, the inconsequential mood changes and the movement of the conversation in an illogical series of semi-circles and tangents, which is as much Chekhovian as Ibsenian.[1] Miller's deftness of touch in rendering the flavour of provincial life is also reminiscent of Chekhov.

It is Ibsenian, of course, as Miller has himself said in the Introduction to his Collected Plays, in the sense that the story is nearly over before the action starts. Much of the time has

---

1. The Russian playwright and short-story writer Anton Chekhov (1860–1904) and Norwegian playwright Henrik Ibsen (1828–1906) were among the most influential realist writers of the nineteenth century.

therefore to be spent in bringing the past into the present. But what is remarkable is how neatly Miller does this, and it is worth analysing the construction in some detail.

ALL MY SONS' ARTFUL CONSTRUCTION

We notice the broken apple tree the moment the lights come up but Joe Keller is half-way through his conversation with his neighbour Frank before they talk about last night's storm which blew it down. Even the tree has been called an Ibsenian symbol but its main function is to introduce the plot as it does when Frank talks about it as 'Larry's tree' and mentions that he is working on Larry's horoscope. After this it is easy for Miller to start planting the play's prehistory. Joe's son Larry, a pilot, was reported missing during the war, three years ago, and Kate, his mother, still refuses to believe that he is dead.

Another neighbour, Dr Jim Bayliss, and his overweight wife, Sue, who never lets him out of her sight for longer than she can help, let us know that there is a beautiful girl in the house. Ann, who was Larry's fiancée, is staying with the Kellers at the invitation of Chris, the younger son, and we learn from Frank's wife, Lydia, that they are living in the house which used to belong to Ann's father.

But we do not get any more of the plot yet. First we have a lot of banter. After Chris, who wants to read the book-section of the Sunday paper, has teased his father about his ignorance, we see Joe rather charmingly playing policemen with Jim's young son, kidding the boy into believing that there is a jail inside the house. It is only then that Chris, who wants to marry Ann, tries to get his father to side with him in the fight this is bound to involve with Kate, who still thinks of Ann as Larry's fiancée. We also get our first focus on two very important points: the closeness of the relationship between Joe and Chris, and the difference between their attitudes to the family business. . . .

Kate's appearance immediately shows how hard the fight is going to be. In the earlier drafts of the play she was the dominant character and there was a great stress on her belief in astrology. Though Miller later shifted the main focus to the father-son relationship, Kate remains a dominating personality and she has the first speech in which the language rises above the pedestrian level of chat, argument and wisecracks. There is a lyrical rhetoric in her description of the dream from which she awoke to see the tree break and the mercury in Chris's rhetorical thermometer jumps in response. . . .

Again, when she is left alone with Joe, the rhythm in Kate's speeches and the slight but significant deviations from natural conversational syntax give Kate a formidable impressiveness. Her stupidity and her stubborn superstitiousness come almost to seem like a dignified refusal to be bound by the norms of reasonableness.

When Jim's young son comes back, she gets very worked up about the jail game Joe is playing with him.

MOTHER: Go home, Bert. [BERT *turns around and goes up drive-way. She is shaken. Her speech is bitten off, extremely urgent.*] I want you to stop that, Joe. That whole jail business!

KELLER [*alarmed, therefore angered*]: Look at you, look at you shaking.

MOTHER [*trying to control herself, moving about clasping her hands*]: I can't help it.

KELLER: What have I got to hide? What the hell is the matter with you, Kate?

MOTHER: I didn't say you had anything to hide, I'm just telling you to stop it! Now stop it!

But almost before his denial can make the suspicion dawn in our minds that maybe he has got something to hide, Ann has come out on the porch and good-natured banter is resumed. Until, rather mystifyingly, the theme of her father is introduced.

MOTHER: Your mother—she's not getting a divorce, heh?

ANN: No, she's calmed down about it now. I think when he gets out they'll probably live together. In New York, of course.

MOTHER: That's fine, because your father is still—I mean he's a decent man after all is said and done.

ANN: I don't care. She can take him back if she likes.

The conversation switches to Larry and Ann denies that she is waiting for him. It is when the tactless Frank comes on that we find out Steve, her father, is in prison. . . .

We now see how cleverly Miller has prepared the ground for this revelation with the game about the jail and Kate's reaction to it. The ensuing conversation makes it clear that Joe was in partnership with Steve and narrowly escaped going to prison himself after they had sold cracked cylinder heads to the Army Air Force, causing twenty-one planes to crash in Australia. . . .

All we know now though is that Ann, who thinks her father is the guilty one, does not allow herself to pity him or go on loving him. . . .

All seems to be going well between Chris and Ann, but her brother George, a lawyer, who has never before visited their father in prison, has been there today and is now on the telephone to say that he is on his way over. Ann goes in to speak to him and Joe's nervousness reminds us of his 'What have I got to hide?' Kate obviously shares his anxiety and the act ends on a note of suspenseful foreboding when she warns him that he will now have to be smart.

THE USE OF MINOR CHARACTERS

The bitchy Sue is well used at the beginning of Act Two. After a superficially friendly chat with Ann she asks her not to settle down with Chris in the neighbourhood because of the effect he has on her husband.

> SUE: Jim's a successful doctor. But he's got an idea he'd like to do medical research. Discover things. You see?
>
> ANN: Well, isn't that good?
>
> SUE: Research pays twenty-five dollars a week minus laundering the hair-shirt. You've got to give up your life to go into it.
>
> ANN: How does Chris—
>
> SUE [*with growing feeling*]: Chris makes people want to be better than it's possible to be. He does that to people.

And towards the end of the conversation she contributes usefully towards the build-up to the *scène à faire*[2] to come when she throws away the line:

> Everybody knows Joe pulled a fast one to get out of jail.

When Chris comes out, Ann passes on the doubt about Joe and when Joe comes out, after some pleasant ragging, he increases our suspicions by offering Ann to set George up with some friends of his in a local legal practice and to help Steve by taking him back into the business when he comes out of prison. When Chris objects, the tension mounts, only to be relaxed immediately when the gentle Lydia comes on to help arrange Kate's hair for the party they are planning for the evening. But it is pulled sharply taut again when Jim, who has driven George from the station, rushes in to warn

---

2. A scene where a major confrontation takes place.

the others not to let him in, saying that Kate is in no fit state to have this 'exploded in front of her'.

George comes in under his own steam and ominously recoils from physical contact with Chris and with Ann. The storm seems about to break when Ann notices he is wearing a hat.

GEORGE: Your father's—He asked me to wear it.

ANN: How is he?

GEORGE: He got smaller.

ANN: Smaller?

GEORGE: Yeah, little. [*Holds out his hand to measure.*] He's a little man. That's what happens to suckers, you know. It's good I went to him in time—another year there'd be nothing left but his smell.

Peremptorily George tells her she is not going to marry Chris. Ann tries to soothe him but he bursts out with the story. On the crucial day, Joe had stayed at home pretending to be sick and given Steve instructions over the telephone to cover over the cracks in the cylinder heads.

When Kate comes out, all is sweetness again on the surface while underneath it the question of whether Ann and Chris believe George's story remains unanswered. George responds readily to Kate's warmth, and the reappearance of Lydia—all four neighbours are very adroitly exploited—reminds him painfully of the chance of marrying her that he has missed. Kate shows her solidarity with Joe in preparing the ground for the bribe he has up his sleeve for George and she even adds a bribe of her own: she will find a girl for him. The banter this provokes makes a fizzing cocktail mixture with the tension.

When Joe comes out, he is strained but George is gentle. It seems quite possible he will not force a showdown and he may even submit to their concerted wooing of him. It is a casual remark of Joe's about never having had a day's sickness in his life which seems about to precipitate a climax. But it is averted by Frank's untimely entrance with Larry's horoscope. And when he goes, it becomes a different climax from the one we expect. Kate tries to make Ann leave with George. She flatly refuses unless Chris tells her to go. Chris only tells George to go and when Ann supports Chris, George meekly obeys, perhaps a little implausibly after his earlier show of ferocious indignation.

It is through Kate that Miller tries to weld the two themes together:

> MOTHER: Your brother's alive, darling, because if he's dead your father killed him. Do you understand me now? As long as you live, that boy is alive. God does not let a son be killed by his father. Now you see, don't you? Now you see.

And when Chris confronts Joe with a direct accusation, his apologia merges the business ethic of survival into his love for his son:

> KELLER: You're a boy, what could I do! I'm in business, a man is in business; a hundred and twenty cracked, you're out of business; you got a process, the process don't work you're out of business; you don't know how to operate, your staff is no good; they close you up, they tear up your contracts, what the hell's it to them? You lay forty years into a business and they knock you out in five minutes, what could I do, let them take forty years, let them take my life away? [*His voice cracking.*] I never thought they'd install them. I swear to God. I thought they'd stop 'em before anybody took off.
>
> CHRIS: Then why'd you ship them out?
>
> KELLER: By the time they could spot them I thought I'd have the process going again, and I could show them they needed me and they'd let it go by. But weeks passed and I got no kick-back, so I was going to tell them.
>
> CHRIS: Then why didn't you tell them?
>
> KELLER: It was too late. The paper, it was all over the front page, twenty-one went down, it was too late. They came with handcuffs into the shop, what could I do? [*He sits on bench.*] Chris . . . Chris, I did it for you, it was a chance and I took it for you. I'm sixty-one years old, when would I have another chance to make something for you? Sixty-one years old you don't get another chance, do ya?

THE FAILURE OF LANGUAGE

Chris's passionate retort makes an effective curtain, but the rhetorical language is something of a let-down.

> CHRIS [*with burning fury*]: For me! Where do you live, where have you come from? For me!—I was dying every day and you were killing my boys and you did it for me? What the hell do you think I was thinking of, the goddam business? Is that as far as your mind can see, the business? What is that, the world—the business? What the hell do you mean, you did it for me? Don't you have a country? Don't you live in the world? What the hell are you? You're not even an animal, no animal kills his own, what are you? What must I do to you? I ought to tear the tongue out of your mouth, what must I do? [*With*

his fist he pounds down upon his father's shoulder. He stumbles away, covering his face as he weeps.] What must I do, Jesus God, what must I do?

KELLER: Chris . . . My Chris . . .

Again at the beginning of Act Three, the neighbours are skillfully used. It is two o'clock in the morning and Jim comes in from an emergency operation to find Kate still rocking in her chair on the porch waiting for Chris. Again the language is disappointing as Jim tries to reassure her.

JIM: Oh, no, he'll come back. We all come back, Kate. These private little revolutions always die. The compromise is always made. In a peculiar way, Frank is right—every man does have a star. The star of one's honesty. And you spend your life groping for it, but once it's out it never lights again. I don't think he went very far. He probably just wanted to be alone to watch his star go out.

The simplicity of Joe's language when he talks about the family is much more acceptable. It is what we expect from him.

KELLER: There's nothin' he could do that I wouldn't forgive. Because he's my son. Because I'm his father and he's my son.

MOTHER: Joe, I tell you—

KELLER: Nothin's bigger than that. And you're goin' to tell him, you understand? I'm his father and he's my son, and if there's something bigger than that I'll put a bullet in my head!

Altogether, the situation is far more brilliantly contrived than the speeches and Ann is given two excellent trumps. First she offers to keep silent about Joe if Kate will agree to her marriage with Chris, and when Kate's stubbornness proves stronger even than her concern for her husband, Ann plays her ace—Larry's letter. Kate moans as she reads it but it is not read out loud until after Chris has come back, intending to go away on his own.

CHRIS: I could jail him! I could jail him, if I were human any more. But I'm like everybody else now. I'm practical now. You made me practical.

MOTHER: But you have to be.

CHRIS: The cats in that alley are practical, the bums who ran away when we were fighting were practical. Only the dead ones weren't practical. But now I'm practical, and I spit on myself. I'm going away. I'm going now.

ANN [*going up to him*]: I'm coming with you.

CHRIS: No, Ann.

ANN: Chris, I don't ask you to do anything about Joe.

CHRIS: You do, you do.

ANN: I swear I never will.

CHRIS: In your heart you always will.

ANN: Then do what you have to do!

CHRIS: Do what? What is there to do? I've looked all night for a reason to make him suffer.

ANN: There's reason, there's reason!

CHRIS: What? Do I raise the dead when I put him behind bars? Then what'll I do it for? We used to shoot a man who acted like a dog, but honour was real there, you were protecting something. But here? This is the land of the great big dogs, you don't love a man here, you eat him! That's the principle; the only one we live by—it just happened to kill a few people this time, that's all. The world's that way, how can I take it out on him? What sense does that make? This is a zoo, a zoo!

Again the language is too banal and flat to reach the level of intensity required by the situation. The situation carries it theatrically but it does not justify the way Chris accepts Joe's attempt to shift the blame on to the capitalist system. Chris is much too much of an idealist, a lover of mankind to agree, even in this mood, that Joe is no worse than most men.

KELLER: Who worked for nothin' in that war? When they work for nothin', I'll work for nothin'. Did they ship a gun or a truck outa Detroit before they got their price? Is that clean? It's dollars and cents, nickels and dimes; war and peace, it's nickels and dimes, what's clean? Half the goddam country is gotta go if I go! That's why you can't tell me.

CHRIS: That's exactly why.

KELLER: Then . . . why am *I* bad?

CHRIS: *I* know you're no worse than most men but I thought you were better. I never saw you as a man. I saw you as my father.

THE PLAY ENDS WITH A BLURRED FOCUS

The theme of filial love is blurring the moral focus. It is the moral condemnation from his other son, who crashed his plane out of shame, that drives Joe to a change of heart. He says he will give himself up to the police.

MOTHER: You're so foolish. Larry was your son too, wasn't he? You know he'd never tell you to do this.

KELLER [*looking at letter in his hand*]: Then what is this if it isn't telling me? Sure, he was my son. But I think to him they

were all my sons. And I guess they were, I guess they were.
I'll be right down. [*Exits into house.*]

Once inside the house he shoots himself, which produces a
highly theatrical curtain without making the change of heart
theatrically valid. It is always hard to dramatize a profound
inner change in a play in which plot and situation are contrived as tightly as they are here—unless the language is poetic. Which is not, of course, to say that it needs to be written
in verse. Ibsen, [Swedish dramatist August] Strindberg and
Chekhov all filtered poetry from the situation into prose dialogue. And in *Death of a Salesman* so did Arthur Miller.

CHAPTER 4

Characters

READINGS ON
ALL MY SONS

Generational Conflict in *All My Sons*

Dinkar Burathoki

The struggle of the son to free himself from his father so that he might realize his individuality is as old as the Bible and the world of the ancient Greeks. This archetypal struggle also characterizes the early work of Arthur Miller, especially in *All My Sons* and the play that followed, *Death of a Salesman* (1949). In this psychological interpretation of *All My Sons*, Dinkar Burathoki maintains that Chris Keller's struggle to individuate himself means that he must reject his attitude of devotion, awe, and love for Joe Keller and see his father for the flawed individual he truly is.

Arthur Miller is the only surviving avant-garde writer of modern American drama. He is also the most respected critic of drama today. His plays have presented a critical consciousness of the times with realistic insight coupled with a cynic's perception—qualities which have made it possible for him to expose the obsessions, compulsive neuroses, power- and success-drives so integral a part of the American milieu. He is, as [critic] Bamber Gascoigne says, "an intellectual craftsman who will take any challenging subject and make a play of it."

Critics have dubbed his plays "social plays", "domestic tragedies" or even "moral commentaries", but Miller firmly adheres to the belief that his purpose of writing plays was "to tell a truth already known but unrecognised as such". About his own style, he confesses:

> I had tried to make it on the stage by writing wonder. But wonder had betrayed me and the only other cause I had was the one I took—to seek cause and effect, hard actions, facts, the geometry of relationships, . . . to let the wonder rise up like a mist, a gas, or vapor from the gradual and remorseless crush of factual and psychological conflict.

Some of the themes of his plays which outline his realism

Excerpted from "Father-Son Relationships in Miller's Plays," by Dinkar Burathoki in *Perspectives on Arthur Miller*, edited by Atma Ram. Copyright © 1988 by Atma Ram. Reprinted with permission from Abhinav Publications.

and his social concern are: the American dream of success, and wealth; the assertion of one's identity; the materialistically instigated social traumas that lead to the abandonment of moral scruples and intelligence; the loneliness and despair of an individual in a dehumanised society: marital relationship, sexual morality; and the most recurrent motif—the conflicting father-son relationship. This last motif occurs in the first two successful plays *All My Sons* (1947), *Death of a Salesman* (1949), and in *The Price* (1968).

THE FATHER'S AUTHORITY AND THE SON'S EGO

Arthur Miller, commenting on the instability of the family structure, is quoted as saying, "How may man make for himself a home in that vastness of strangers, and how may he transform that vastness into a home?" The greatest obstacle, which he finds in the way of family solidarity, is the authority of the father which confronts the ego of the son, "Be it Tolstoy, Dostoyevsky, Hemingway, you, or I, we are formed in this world when we are sons and daughters and the first truths we know throw us into conflict with our fathers and mothers." This realisation must have dawned on him quite early in his life, because, we are certainly aware of the autobiographical nature of his works; and, early in his writing career when he was struggling with *The Man Who Had All the Luck* he discovered how a "simple shift of relationships" could change ordinary plays into great ones:

> The play was impossible to fix because the overt story was only tangential to the secret drama its author was quite unconsciously trying to write. But in the writing of the father-son relationship and of the son's search for his relatedness there was a fullness of feeling I had never known before; a crescendo was struck with a force I could almost touch.

The fragile nature of the American family was a poignant social problem, especially during the Depression years, when Arthur Miller grew up in a family that was ruined by it. [Critic] Irving Jacobson, in his study of Miller's story "I Don't Need You Any More", refers to the important family motifs in Miller's works:

> ... the failures of fathers are of a personal or an economic nature ... conflicts between education and family loyalty, and recurrent figures, such as the mother who was forced into a marriage that aborted her possibilities for personal development, the ill-educated father who has become exhausted into inadequacy, the "good" brother whose own sense of virtue

binds him to the family in contrast to a less virtuous brother whose actions and discoveries force him away from the family.

FATHERHOOD AND SUCCESS

The cut-throat competition in trade and business, uncertainty about the future, and the keen struggle for existence, emphasised and heightened the success myth of America. Each individual was required to prove his ability at a young age and the parents did not protect their adolescents for being liabilities on them. . . . In such a competitive capitalistic society, the parents expected to see their children contributing to the family resources, and the sons wanted to pursue their own ideals, which resulted in tension. The hysterical compulsion towards success broke the backbone of the established conservative American family. . . .

The conflict between the father and son is presented as a conflict of their two contrasting viewpoints. Both the father and the son have their alter egos to present a correct picture. In *All My Sons*, Joe Keller has Deever; in *Death of a Salesman*, Willy has Charley or Ben, and Biff and Happy have Bernard; in *The Price*, Father has Solomon and Victor has Walter. The dichotomy has perhaps always existed in Miller himself, his father having betrayed him in the pursuit of his intellectual aims, forcing him to take up jobs demanding physical strength. His brother was also forced into business by his father. Arthur Miller identified more with Arthur M. Rowe, who taught him playwriting at Michigan University and helped him become a successful dramatist. Similarly, Chris considers his father a predator; out to destroy his own race, and the guilt of servitude to such malicious designs for self-aggrandisement makes him hate his father and his sympathies are on Deever's side because he has suffered for some egocentric's fault.

A SON'S IDEALISM

To understand the dynamics of the father-son relationship, it is necessary for us to consider how the psychic attitudes are formed during the formative years of every individual. The final personality that emerges belongs mostly to the dream-world which each individual inhabits. [Philosopher] Erich Fromm says that "all men are idealists and cannot help being idealists, provided we mean by idealism the striving for the satisfaction of needs which are specifically human and transcend the physiological needs of the individual." Each individual lives in a world of his own in which he is the king. He follows a path of self-determination of right and wrong, good or bad, which has been developed during the formative years as a result of his unique experience. He chooses the course of stability, security and ease, and jealously guards against its collapse. This is known as the individuation process and is directly or indirectly affected by the objective world. He imitates and emulates people who appeal to his own concept of functioning and values and rejects with a subjective bias everything contrary to it. The moment blockades spring up on this course, a compulsive neurosis, an overcompensatory attitude, is developed leading to complex formations which are disruptive in nature. "A complex", according to [psychologist Carl] Jung, "is a typical energy configuration which is activated by a situation and problem, both outer or inner, by people, emotional conflicts, maturational needs, etc. It impresses its force pattern upon the totality of happenings within its scope." The concretisation or actualisation of these complexes in the ego-consciousness, whatever has been actualised, tends to become fixed and permanent, even rigid, as an essential part of our ego. The stronger the drive, the more it becomes identified with the "conscious reactive capacity", triggering a defence mechanism which creates a very subjective attitude thus curtailing a man's free choice.

During the adolescent stage an individual is trying to assert his own ego-identity and the parents provide the primary source of inspiration and attitudes. The unconditional love of the mother develops in the adult the qualities of feeling, tenderness, sacrifice and tolerance, whereas identification with the father (super-ego) impresses upon the individual the qualities of drive, domination, authority, reason and aggression. If these qualities are not actualised in the ego-personality, the adult feels alienated and inferior; seeking substitutes for parents in other people. This is called transference. . . .

Since the parents cannot strike a balance in their affection to and training of their children, the self-image of the individual lacks sufficient ego-strength. This fostered person will live in a dream-world having inertia, inflation and lack of adaptation to reality, just as a child not loved by his parents will have an inferiority complex, a strong power-drive and aggressiveness, and over-independence. The attempt

[here] will be to study the father-son relationship, focusing on the psychodynamics from this perspective.

JOE KELLER AND STEVE DEEVER ARE DUAL FATHER FIGURES

All My Sons (1947) is about the avaricious, egocentric industrialist, Joe Keller, who sacrifices the welfare of mankind and his own son's life for his family's welfare, by selling faulty cylinder heads to the government which leads to the death of twenty-one pilots. Knowing fully well that the sale is unethical, he goes ahead with it and when he is asked by Deever to bear the responsibility, he pretends sickness, saving himself from imprisonment and his family from financial trouble. In the process, Deever (Joe's partner) is arrested and the mother and her daughter, Ann, leave the neighbourhood to settle in New York with her son, George, who is a lawyer. Joe Keller and Deever present two aspects of parental and social responsibility. Joe does everything for the family, in the process resorting to socially unethical means of growing rich. He represents the modern industrialist craving for wealth at the cost of others. Deever is morally concerned with the illegal sale and willingly goes to prison when Joe lets him down. He sacrifices the family for "all his sons". Both these attitudes, the selfish family man and the family man with a sense of social responsibility, are justified in their approach towards life. Miller tries to bring out the questions of the individual's self-centredness and his social obligations. A selfish man will remain a threat to society and someone will have to see to it that such cankers are uprooted to save humanity.

CHRIS KELLER'S INDIVIDUATION

Chris and George, and Ann and Larry represent the dichotomy in the attitudes of the children towards their parents. Chris is quite happy in the family set-up because he is being well-provided for and is also going to inherit the business. Even if he knows that his father has used foul means to make his fortune, he does not object to it, because he knows that Larry is dead. His desire to marry Ann (who is Larry's girl) springs from this notion. But, he feels chained whenever he has to do something for himself (like marrying Ann). He says, "I don't know why it is, but everytime I reach out for something I want, I have to pull back because other people will suffer. My whole bloody life, time after time after time".

When he has decided once and for all to marry Ann, he shows that he is going to rebel against his father and also break the illusion of his mother, that her elder son will return. By doing this he knows he is going to act selfishly at the expense of the family and Joe's response is, "all right but—but don't think like that. Because what the hell did I work for? That's only for you. Chris, the whole shootin' match is for you." To which Chris replies, "Then help me stay here".

Chris chooses the course of life in which he is secure and hence the question of marrying the girl he loves (although she is perhaps the only girl he has met, and even Kate is critical of the match). To satisfy his selfish motive, he is also willing to shatter his mother's belief that Larry is still alive after being missing for three years. When the story of how Joe has let down Steve Deever is revealed, his respect and moral attitude towards his father is shattered. This provokes the morality of Chris, who refuses to be a party to his father's crime, and it also initiates his individuation process. He decides and threatens to go away with Ann when she reveals through Larry's letter that he (Larry) has actually committed suicide. The image of his father that he had in his mind becomes tarnished. Everything seems to stink of the blood of the 21 pilots who died and also Larry. As [director and critic] Harold Clurman has said of the father-son relationship in Miller's plays:

> The father in Miller's work is a recurrent figure regarded with awe, devotion, love, even when he is proved lamentably fallible and when submission to him becomes painfully questionable. . . . In the crucial confrontation with his father Chris reveals himself (and Miller) by exclaiming, "I know you're no worse than most men but I thought you were better. I never saw you as a man. I saw you as a father." In this he has moved beyond the realm of common sense and speaks of fatherhood in a religious sense.

This "religious sense" . . . makes the son look up to his father with awe and devotion and makes the son believe that his father's is the only right attitude towards life (which he has learned, during his formative years). In Freudian and Jungian psychology the quest for self-assertion requires from the individual the breaking of the magical bond with the mother and the "killing" (not physically, but psychically) of the father. Chris, by forcing Joe to suicide and shattering the illusion of his mother, seeks the way towards his self-assertion.

The Emotional Costs of Denial

Steven R. Centola

Arthur Miller witnessed World War II and the Holocaust. Steven R. Centola maintains that this may have
influenced *All My Sons*: Joe Keller's refusal to acknowledge his involvement in his own "war crime"
reflects how many Germans immediately after the
war reacted to Hitler's crimes against humanity. Like
many Germans in the aftermath of World War II, Joe
Keller sees himself as a victim of powerful forces beyond his control—an evasion of personal responsibility that is contemptuously dismissed by his son Chris.
Yet the Kellers and their neighbors are implicated in
Joe Keller's denial, illustrating the extent to which denial's destructive effects can take over an entire community. Centola is a professor of drama and American literature at Millersville University in
Pennsylvania. He is also the founder and president of
the Arthur Miller Society.

Winner of the New York Drama Critics' Circle Award for best
play of 1947, *All My Sons* is the work that launched Arthur
Miller's long and distinguished career in the theatre. While
few would argue that it is Miller's best or most important
play, no one would dispute the fact that *All My Sons* deserves
a special place in the playwright's canon because it constitutes his first major theatrical achievement, displays his extraordinary skill in handling dramatic form, and presages
even better things yet to come from one of America's greatest dramatists. . . .

　As he wrote *All My Sons*, he knew that the play would explore the way in which choices and behavior in the past im-
pinge upon, shape, and even give rise to unforeseen and in-
escapable consequences in the future. For Miller discovered

Excerpted from *"All My Sons,"* by Steven R. Centola in *The Cambridge Companion to
Arthur Miller,* edited by Christopher Bigsby. Copyright © 1997 by Cambridge University Press. Reprinted with permission from Cambridge University Press.

early on the structural principle that he would repeatedly return to as a playwright—a principle that he has aphoristically stated throughout his career by saying: "the structure of a play is always the story of how the birds came home to roost." In *All My Sons*, Miller builds and reveals dramatic action that, by its very movement—by its creation, suspension, and resolution of tension; its inexorable rush toward tragic confrontation—proves that the past is always present and cannot be ignored, forgotten, or denied. . . .

ALL MY SONS' UNIVERSAL RICHNESS

While one could discuss [the] central theme in *All My Sons* exclusively in terms of its social context and its call for socially responsible behavior, reducing the play and Miller's treatment of this issue to these terms alone fails to do justice to its complexity and fascinating exploration of universally significant questions about the enigmatic nature of the self's relation to others. . . .

Ultimately, *All My Sons* is a play about both paradox and denial—or to state it more precisely, it is about a theme that Miller has described as "the paradox of denial." In his autobiography, Miller discusses the circumstances that led to his systematic exploration of this theme while developing the character Maggie in *After the Fall*:[1]

> It was after returning from Germany that I began to feel committed to the new play, possibly because its theme—the paradox of denial—seemed so eminently the theme of Germany, and Germany's idealistically denied brutality emblematic of the human dilemma in our time. . . . And so, bewildered and overwhelmed, she secretly came to side against herself, taking the world's part as its cynicism toward her ground down her brittle self-regard, until denial finally began its work, leaving her all but totally innocent of insight into her own collaboration as well as her blind blows of retaliation. . . . The complex process of denial in the great world thus reflected in an individual seemed a wonderfully illuminating thematic center . . .

While he may not have had the benefit of observing the Nuremberg Trials at the time he wrote *All My Sons*, he did witness the Second World War and was fully aware of the crimes against humanity evident in the Holocaust. Perhaps this background to the drama had as much to do with his writing a play about a guilty individual's betrayal of trust through war-profiteering crimes as the Nuremberg Trials and

1. *After the Fall* was first performed in 1964.

Germany's denial had later on his creation of *After the Fall.*

Beyond such speculation, however, other factors justify applying Miller's comments about Maggie and *After the Fall* to Joe Keller and *All My Sons.* Even though they differ stylistically, both plays are about choices and the paradox inherent in making choices. The paradox Miller describes in his Foreword to *After the Fall* is also evident in *All My Sons*:

> there [is] . . . always the choice, always the conflict between his own needs and the desires and the impediments others put in his way. Always, and from the beginning, the panorama of human beings raising up in him and in each other the temptation of the final solution to the problem of being a self at all— the solution of obliterating whatever stands in the way, thus destroying what is loved as well.

JOE KELLER'S ILLUSIONS AND HIS ANGUISH

The crimes against society committed by Joe Keller derive from the same instinct for self-preservation and self-assertion that foster the adoption of a counterfeit innocence and the illusion of one's being a victim at the hands of others. Like Maggie, Keller prefers to see himself as a victim of others. Instead of acknowledging his complicity in the crime that sends unsuspecting pilots to their deaths, he lies about his involvement and denies his personal culpability so that he can preserve his false image of himself and maintain the illusion that he has regained his rightful place in society. Like Maggie, Keller denies his connection to the disaster because he blinds himself to the impulses that make him a danger to himself as well as to others. Keller cannot face what Miller calls "the murder in him, the sly and everlasting complicity with the forces of destruction." For this reason, Miller says, "Joe Keller's trouble, in a word, is not that he cannot tell right from wrong but that his cast of mind cannot admit that he, personally, has any viable connection with his world, his universe, or his society." Hence, *All My Sons* "lays siege to . . . the fortress of unrelatedness" and shows why an individual's betrayal of trust and refusal to accept responsibility for others, if left uncensured by society, "can mean a jungle existence for all of us . . ." Paradoxically, the very denial that is designed to protect him from prosecution and incarceration sets in motion the chain of events that lead to Keller's own self-imprisonment and self-imposed execution. Therefore, the paradox of denial in *All My Sons* is that not only does denial dehumanize, by nullifying the value of the social contract through the justification of indefensible anti-social acts, but it also intensifies the personal anguish and the irremediable alienation that plunge an individual into despair and bring about his tragic suicide.

Keller's anguish is in evidence throughout much of the play. He appears both "shamed" and "alarmed" early in Act One when his wife, Kate, reprimands him for telling children in the neighborhood that he has a jail hidden in his basement. Defensively snapping, "What have I got to hide?" Keller suggests not only that he begrudges Kate's condescending treatment of him, but also that he resents her veiled reminder that he does, indeed, have something to hide. The jail reference is repeated throughout the play to bring the past into the present and thereby strengthen the association between Keller's crime and his guilt. This motif underlines the fact that Keller's actions have consequences while also serving to illustrate the problem of setting oneself apart from and above the outer world. As though he were confined in a jail, Keller views the world as having "a forty-foot front . . . [that] ended at the building line." He denies his relation to society so that he can excuse unethical business practices that keep his manufacturing company fiscally sound and his family financially secure. So long as he acts to preserve the welfare of his family, Keller believes that anything he does can be justified. He convinces himself that his sole responsibility in life is to be successful so that he can support his wife and children. For Keller, "Nothin' is bigger" than the family.

Even the setting of the play is designed to reveal and comment on Keller's myopic world view. The entire play takes place in the *"back yard of the Keller home. . . . The stage is hedged on right and left by tall, closely planted poplars which lend the yard a secluded atmosphere."* This scenic image successfully augments the stage action as gradual disclosures of family secrets and repressed feelings surface in the dialogue.

OUR UNDERLYING SHAME AND GUILT

Miller skillfully works exposition into the plot that increases dramatic tension while simultaneously disclosing incriminating clues about Keller's guilt. For example, while reminiscing about his trial and the day he was released from prison, Keller describes himself parading in front of his neighbors after being exonerated and intentionally suffering their accusing stares while holding "a court paper in [his] pocket to prove" his innocence. As George Deever, the embittered son of Keller's incarcerated partner, later tells the Keller family, the court paper really proves nothing since Keller won his trial on a technicality: the prosecution simply could not prove conclusively that Keller ordered his partner over the telephone to conceal the cracks and sell the faulty equipment. Nevertheless, by acting as if the court paper were proof of his innocence, Keller denies any connection to the crime and to the community whose trust he has violated. His denial of personal culpability shows not only his complete lack of remorse, but also his complete unwillingness to face the consequences of his actions. Paradoxically, by suggesting that only his possession of a court paper proves his innocence, Keller also unconsciously incriminates himself, for the audience knows that his innocence should derive solely from his awareness of the inaccuracy of the accusation against him. Keller's denial, therefore, has the opposite effect on his audience that it is designed to achieve.

Later, when Keller pleads with his son, Chris, to take his money and use it "without shame . . . with joy," Keller again unwittingly reveals his guilt. He knows that he has used unsavory means to build his fortune and that his son would have nothing to do with the family business if he knew that it prospered only because of the death of innocent pilots. Fearing that George Deever and his sister, Ann, will reveal the truth and turn Chris away from him, Keller tries to convince his son that the fortune earned is "good money, there's nothing wrong with that money." His insistence again produces unanticipated results. Instead of gaining Chris's confidence, Keller arouses his suspicion as Chris backs away from such unwanted suggestive conversation. The performance didascalia—"*a little frightened*"––that characterize Chris's apprehension over his father's unctuous appeal suggest that he is hesitant to understand too fully the implication of his father's entreaty. Like his father, Chris initially shows little interest in testing the strength of the bonds of family relationships with the uncomfortable truth.

JOE KELLER FALSELY SEES HIMSELF AS A VICTIM

When the truth about his role in the crime is finally revealed in Act Two, Keller tries to mitigate his guilt by portraying himself as the victim of forces beyond his control. He has convinced himself, and futilely tries to persuade Chris, that, given the limited choices available at the time, he made the best choice possible:

> I'm in business, a man is in business; a hundred and twenty cracked, you're out of business; you got a process, the process don't work you're out of business; you don't know how to operate, your stuff is no good; they close you up, they tear up your contracts, what the hell's it to them? You lay forty years into a business and they knock you out in five minutes, what could I do, let them take forty years, let them take my life away?

Keller first tries to rationalize the crime by explaining that he only let the defective machinery leave the shop because he hoped the parts would perform satisfactorily. However, after Chris forces him to admit that he knew the planes were likely to crash with the faulty engines, Keller justifies his decision by pretending that it was consonant with the code of ethics prevalent in American business transactions during the war:

> Who worked for nothin' in that war? When they work for nothin', I'll work for nothin'. Did they ship a gun or a truck outa Detroit before they got their price? Is that clean? It's dollars and cents, nickels and dimes; war and peace, it's nickels and dimes, what's clean? Half the Goddam country is gotta go if I go!

Instead of assuaging his guilt and restoring his son's lost respect and love, Keller's denial of wrongdoing only serves to exacerbate the family crisis and intensify his anguish and alienation. . . .

KATE KELLER MUST SHARE RESPONSIBILITY

One of the playwright's trademarks is his uncompromising honesty in the investigation of the role each person plays in his own tragedy. Much of the success of *All My Sons* has to do with Miller's complex vision of the Kellers' shared guilt and complicity in the family's collapse. For Joe Keller is not solely responsible for the Keller family's troubles. Like her husband, Kate also lives in denial and resorts to lies and self-deception as a means of contending with her anguish and sorrow. Unable to accept the death of her elder son, Larry, in the war, Kate deludes herself into believing that he is still alive and will one day return home. To fortify her conviction, she adopts a blind faith in religion and obstinately argues that "God does not let a son be killed by his father." Beyond all reason, she also succumbs to a superstitious reliance on astrology and maintains that Larry's horoscope contradicts everyone's suspicion that he died in the war. Kate prefers to believe that external forces—the stars—determine her son's destiny and not individual free choice. She futilely tries to deceive herself into believing that Larry could not deliberately crash his plane in a sincere effort to atone for his father's criminal act. However, when Ann Deever produces the incriminating letter from Larry that explains the motive for his suicide, Kate suffers no terrific shock. She has always known, while constantly denying, that Larry had died in the war.

Kate also plays a significant role in the cover-up of her husband's war-profiteering crime. Instead of encouraging him to face his responsibilities honestly, she protects him from prosecution by falsely verifying his lie. Ironically, however, her loyalty to her husband only serves to widen the gulf between them because their knowledge of their deception makes them feel uncomfortable in each other's presence. Both experience guilt and shame beneath the other's accusing stare. Therefore, by denying the facts and by conspiring to withhold the truth from their community, Joe and Kate Keller sentence themselves to a lonely and unhappy marriage.

THE DUALITY OF CHRIS KELLER

Chris Keller is also responsible for his family's dilemma. The idealistic youth who energetically professes to detest dishonesty is as guilty as his parents of attempting to hide from reality. Though he persists in pushing his mother toward an acceptance of his brother's death, he does so for his own selfish reasons and not because he thinks it is in her best interest to be able to face reality. Likewise, even though he adopts a high moral tone and energetically indicts his father for his criminal irresponsibility, Chris knows that his words ring hollow because he has long suspected his father's guilt but deliberately avoided confronting the truth—again for purely selfish motives. At some level, Chris fears that, if he allows himself to see his father's human imperfections, he will also have to recognize his own limitations—and his experiences in the war make him dread that confrontation.

Having watched heroic young men under his command die selflessly in battle to save their comrades, Chris feels guilty for failing them and surviving the war. His guilt is the guilt of the survivor—the guilt, as Holga tells Quentin in *After the Fall*, that derives from knowing "no one is innocent they did not kill." Chris desperately wants to escape from this guilt and the anguish it produces, so, when given the chance, he tries to find relief by disguising his disgust with himself as contempt for his father. His father becomes his scapegoat, and Chris casts all his own feelings of guilt and self-loathing onto his father in the hope that, by destroying his father, he can somehow expiate his own sins and escape from his own personal torment. It is hard, therefore, not to see and condemn the hypocrisy behind the zeal that leads to Keller's suicide. Miller effectively raises questions about Chris's real motives for bringing his father to justice and suggests that Chris's own denial at least partially accounts for his condemnation of his father. . . .

THE MINOR CHARACTERS' COMPLICITY AND SELFISHNESS

Even minor characters in the play—Ann Deever, Jim Bayliss, and Sue Bayliss, specifically—demonstrate through their denial the adverse and oftentimes ironic effects of dishonest behavior. Like the Kellers, these characters withhold the truth from each other and themselves to sustain their illusions and protect their tenuous happiness. Ann Deever at least suspects Keller's guilt because of the letter she received from Larry before his suicide; however, she refrains from impeaching Keller until she feels compelled to do so in order to save her relationship with Chris. Her motives are selfish, governed primarily by a fundamental drive for self-preservation. Jim and Sue Bayliss also suspect Keller's guilt, yet they relinquish all sense of personal responsibility for ensuring that justice prevails. In fact, they continue to treat the Kellers as their best friends. Sue Bayliss even expresses admiration for Keller for pulling "a fast one to get out of jail." Jim Bayliss goes one step further and tries to protect the Kellers from George Deever's hostile accusations and the family's ultimate confrontation over the truth. His interference, however, speaks loudly of his own insecurities and feeble effort to escape from reality. Jim tries to shield the family, particularly Chris, from the truth not only because he longs to protect them, but also because he needs to sustain the illusion of their perfection. He wants to keep alive the possibility for noble and decent behavior and believes the preservation of the Keller myth achieves this goal. Having already watched "The star of [his] honesty . . . go out," Jim knows he is lost "in the usual darkness." If he no longer has the illusory image of Chris's perfection to drive and inspire him, he will find it impossible "to remember the kind of man [he] wanted to be." Therefore, his denial has the same ironic impact as the self-deception and mendacity of the Keller family. . . .

THE DESTRUCTIVE EFFECTS OF DENIAL

Particularly because of his treatment of the theme of the paradox of denial, Miller's play has a resonance that transcends its contemporary society and immediate situation. The catastrophe that affects the Keller family can occur anytime so long as people choose to embrace a counterfeit innocence that conceals their impulse to betray and dominate others. *All My Sons* proves that Miller's later indictment of Germany during the Nuremberg Trials in *After the Fall* can just as easily apply to any country which fosters illusions that elevate the native populace above the ostensibly menacing and inferior foreigners. In a country at war with an external threat, perhaps it is especially easy to succumb to such self-deception, and in that case, then, the background to *All My Sons* makes the play's drama that much more salient and relevant. . . .

In *All My Sons*, Miller shows how the impulse to betray and to deny responsibility for others, when left ungoverned, can run rampant and wreak havoc on the individual, his family, and his society—even, perhaps, civilization as a whole. The paradox of denial, therefore, is that the very defense mechanism that is employed to justify the rightness of a socially reprehensible act can ultimately become the exclusive means by which an individual self-destructs. The Kellers, and many of those around them, choose to blame everyone else for their dilemma, but only they are the authors of their destiny—and their failure to accept the tremendous burden of their freedom and responsibility is itself the cause of their personal tragedy.

Chris Keller's Failure as a Moral Force

Barry Gross

Chris Keller feels a heightened sense of moral responsibility in *All My Sons* since he bears the guilt of having survived the war while others whom he loved died. Yet unlike his father Joe, who has always known why he acted the way he did, Chris doesn't necessarily practice what he preaches about honoring the dead and living a better life as a returning veteran. For instance, he has chosen to work for his father—a man who made his fortune from the same war in which young men died—even though he professes to hate the business world his father represents. Through Chris Keller, the play advocates the need to acknowledge the larger world that exists beyond the nuclear family; however, one is never sure how deeply Chris himself embraces this position. Therefore, Barry Gross maintains that *All My Sons'* "larger context" is compromised. A specialist on American novelist F. Scott Fitzgerald, Barry Gross is a professor of English at Michigan State University.

Arthur Miller has always maintained that his plays have not been immediately understood, that *After the Fall* was not about Marilyn Monroe and *Incident at Vichy* was not about anti-Semitism, that *A View from the Bridge* was not about longshoremen and *The Crucible* was not about McCarthyism, that *Death of a Salesman* was not about the business world and *All My Sons* was not about war-profiteering. What, then, is *All My Sons* about?

JOE KELLER'S UNREVEALED HISTORY

In 1947 the generation gap was not the cliché it has since become and *All My Sons* is certainly, on one level, about that.

Reprinted from "*All My Sons* and the Larger Context," by Barry Gross, *Modern Drama*, March 1975. Reprinted with permission from *Modern Drama*.

Joe Keller is almost twice his son Chris' age. He is an "uneducated man for whom there is still wonder in many commonly known things," for instance, that new books are published every week or that a man can earn "a living out of . . . old dictionaries." He is the product of a vanished America, of a time when "either you were a lawyer, or a doctor, or you worked in a shop," a time of limited possibilities for someone "put . . . out at ten" to "earn his keep," for someone who learned English in "one year of night-school" and still does not know what "roué" means or that it is French, still says "brooch" when he means "broach."

We can only guess at Joe Keller's history because the kind of play Miller had in mind would, of necessity, exclude it. *All My Sons* was to be a "jurisprudence," and, as Miller says in the introduction to *Collected Plays,*

> when a criminal is arraigned . . . it is the prosecutor's job to symbolize his behavior for the jury so that the man's entire life can be characterized in one way and not in another. The prosecutor does not mention the accused as a dog lover, a good husband and father, a sufferer from eczema, or a man with a habit of chewing tobacco on the left and not the right side of his mouth.

Well and good: Miller is entitled to establish the design for his own work and to be judged according to the terms he proposes. But the jury is also entitled to hear the defense, indeed must hear it if it is to reach a fair verdict, and Joe Keller's unrevealed history *is* his defense. "Where do you live, where do you come from?" Chris asks him, "Don't you have a country? Don't you live in the world? What the hell are you?" The answers lie buried in Joe Keller's past.

Is he an immigrant? The son of an immigrant? If he had to learn English in night-school, does that mean he grew up speaking German? Yiddish? These are not irrelevant questions if Joe Keller's crime is to be understood in human, rather than aberrational, terms, and it is clearly an important part of Miller's design that Keller's crime be seen as a profoundly human one. There are logical answers to Chris' questions; that Chris cannot imagine them is both result and proof of the generation gap that inevitably separates father and son. The gap can be defined by their differing perceptions of and attitudes toward the idea and the reality of community. Joe Keller is guilty of an anti-social crime not out of intent but out of ignorance; his is a crime of omission, not of commission. For him there is no society, and there never has been one. It is not simply that Joe's "mind can see" only "as far as . . . the business" or that for Joe "the business" is "the world." Actually, he does not see as far as that and for him the world is smaller. Where does he live? He lives at home. Does he live in the world? No. Does he have a country? No. What the hell is he? Provider, bread-winner, husband and father. His world is bounded by the picket fence that encloses the suburban back yard in which the play takes place, his commitments and allegiances do not extend beyond its boundaries. He is an engaged man, but not to man or to men, only to his family, more precisely to his sons, not all the sons of the title but the two sons he has fathered.

"In my day," Joe Keller says wistfully, "when you had a son it was an honor." What else "did [he] work for"? That is not an excuse but it is an explanation. It is not that Joe Keller cannot distinguish between right and wrong, it is that his understanding of what is right and what is wrong has been ineluctably determined by the only reality he has ever known. When he advises Ann not to hate her father he begs her to "see it human," and if we fail to see Joe Keller human then we relegate him to that dark other-world where only monsters dwell, safely removed from the world in which we think we live so we do not have to identify with it or admit our own compliance in it. What is right in Joe Keller's ethos—and it *is* an ethos—is the familial obligation, the father's duty to create something for his son. He is not proud of being a self-made man or of his material success, he is proud that he has made something for his son. There is no zealot like a convert and there is probably no more devoted parent than a neglected or an abandoned child. We know that Willy Loman [in *Death of a Salesman*] was abandoned by his father when he was an infant, and that goes far to explain his passionate involvement in his sons' lives. If Joe's father turned him out at age ten, it is not surprising that his first article of faith should be "a father is a father and a son is a son." Impossible as it may be for Chris to understand or appreciate the fact, Joe was keeping that faith when he shipped out the faulty plane parts: "I did it for you, it was a chance and I took it for you. I'm sixty-one years old, when would I have another chance to make something for you? . . . For you, a business for you!" Misguided, yes; malevolent, no, no more so, in intent, than Willy Loman's suicide, Willy's refusal to die empty-handed, Willy's commitment to the paternal obligation as he understands it, Willy's need to express his love for his son in the only way he knows how. Joe "didn't want [the money] that way" any more than Willy wanted it the way he chose, but he had "a family" and for Joe "nothin' is bigger . . . than the family": "There's nothin' he could do that I wouldn't forgive. Because he's my son. Because I'm his father and he's my son. . . . Nothin's bigger than that. . . . I'm his father and he's my son." There is literally no other frame of reference. It is not only that "a man can't be a Jesus in this world," it is that, to Joe, Jesus is irrelevant. Jesus was never a father.

As a change of heart and a change of mind the denouement is, thus, unconvincing. Joe promises to "put a bullet in [his] head . . . if there's something bigger" than family, he reads Larry's letter, agrees that "they were . . . all [his] sons," and shoots himself. Joe Keller has not overthrown sixty years of thinking and feeling in a minute. Like Willy Loman, he goes to his death deluded, dies in the name of his delusion, dies a believer. He knows only that his sons think there is something bigger than family, that he has shamed them, one to the point of suicide, that his sons for whom he has lived consider him an animal and do not want to live in the same world with him. Joe's suicide is less a moral judgment than an act of love. In effect, Joe kills himself so that Chris need not kill *him*self—Chris: "What must I do?"—and because Chris tells him to—Chris: "Now you tell me what you must do." Joe commits his second anti-social crime in the name of the same love that motivated the first.

CHRIS KELLER'S CONFLICT OF RESPONSIBILITY

For Joe Keller there is no conflict beyond the fact that time has passed and values have, at least according to his sons, changed. The conflict in the play is Chris Keller's, not so much between him and his father, or between his generation's and his father's, but within his own generation, within himself. Chris' is the conflict between who and what he is and who and what he wants to be, or thinks he ought to be. He wants to be, or thinks he ought to be, different from his father. Watching his comrades die for each other and for him, he has become aware of "a kind of—responsibility, man to man." Upon returning from the war, he had thought "to bring that on to the earth again like some kind of a monument and everyone would feel it standing there, behind him, and it would make a difference to him." He knows that if he is alive at all "to open the bank-book, to drive the new car, to see the new refrigerator," it is because "of the love a man can have for a man." Yet when Chris returns home he finds "no meaning in it here," finds that "nobody . . . changed at all."

So Chris knows things his father cannot know, and yet he remains his father's son. He will spend his life in a business that "doesn't inspire" him for more than "an hour a day," he will "grub for money all day long," if it can be "beautiful" when he comes home in the evening. The only monument he can think to build is precisely the one his father has constructed: "I want a family, I want some kids, I want to build something I can give myself to. . . . Oh, Annie, Annie, I'm going to make a fortune for you!" In this light, it is not fair for Chris to make other people feel guilty for their "compromises" or for their inability or unwillingness "to be better than it's possible to be." Chris makes no visible efforts to be better than it is possible to be, or even to be as good as it is possible to be. Sue's branding of Chris as hypocrite—"if Chris wants people to put on the hair-shirt let him take off his broadcloth"—is valid. His shame and guilt are meaningless because they do not lead to action. Society's case against Chris Keller is stronger than its case against Joe Keller because Chris knows better. His tendency is to embroider what he obviously thinks of as an unacceptable reality—Ann: "As soon as you get to know somebody you find a distinction for them"—rather than to attempt to transform that reality into something different, something better.

CHRIS KELLER'S CONTRADICTIONS

Chris' self-proclaimed love for his parents is also suspect. "You're the only one I know who loves his parents," Ann exclaims, to which he replies with some self-congratulation, "I know. It went out of style, didn't it?" He thinks his father is "a great guy," he promises his mother he will "protect" them against George's attacks—but Chris' devotion to his father is based on his assumption that "the man is innocent." He could not love a guilty father, not out of moral fastidiousness but out of self-love. If, as George says, Chris has lied to himself about his father's guilt, it is more to deny what he himself is than what his father is. When Biff Loman stumbles and weeps when he discovers at age seventeen that his father is not the god he thought him, we understand that an adolescent has made a painful but inevitable discovery. When Chris Keller, who has been "a killer" in the war, does the same thing at thirty-two, we must conclude that he is responding to some private drama unwinding inside him rather than to the revelation of his father's guilt. Even his mother is surprised that it is "such a shock" to him; she "always had a feeling that in the back of his head . . . Chris almost knew." Jim insists that Chris could not have known because he "would never know how to live with a thing like that," but Jim idolizes Chris, though we never see why, and his testimony is not reliable. Chris has not allowed himself to admit what he knew *because* he would not know how to live with it. Chris will come back, Jim tells Kate, he will make the necessary compromise; he has gone off so he can "be alone to watch . . . the star of [his] honesty . . . go out." The star Chris has gone out to watch flicker and die is not the star of his honesty but the star of his image of himself as honest, not the fact of his innocence but the lie of his innocence which he has persisted in believing. It is not that he *will* compromise himself, it is that he *has* compromised himself, and now he can no longer deny it.

When Chris returns from his vigil he admits that he "suspected his father and . . . did nothing about it," less in the name of love of father, we suspect, than of love of self. Like his brother Larry, Chris could not imagine himself such a man's son, he would not be able to "face anybody" or himself. Joe Keller's sin, it would seem, is not so much that he profited from the war or sold faulty plane parts to the government or indirectly caused the death of twenty-one men, but that, in revealing himself to be no better "than most men," he "broke his son's heart." For Chris "thought" he *was* "better," that distinction he must assign those he knows: "I never saw you as a man. I saw you as my father. I can't look at you this way. I can't look at myself!" An unwittingly illuminating admission: he cannot look at his father as no better than most *because* he cannot look at himself as no better than most; he has never seen his father as a man because he has not wanted to see himself as one. In Act One Sue makes a remark about how uncomfortable it is living next door to the Holy Family and now we know what she means: as long as Joe (Jehovah?) is The Father, Chris (Christ?) is surely the son, by definition. What Chris cannot forgive Joe for is that, by his crime, the father has robbed the son of his "distinction." Chris laments that he is "like everyone else now," meaning he is "practical now" like "the cats in the alley" and "the bums who ran away when we were fighting," meaning he is not "human any more." But the converse is true: he is now and finally human *because* he must admit he is like everybody else. If "only the dead ones weren't practical." Chris has always been practical but has never admitted it. . . . As a survivor, Chris will have to learn to live with his "practicality," which is his loss of innocence, which is his humanity.

We do not see this happen. Chris is allowed to have Miller's final words and to point the moral of the play: "It's not enough . . . to be sorry. . . . You can be better! Once and for all you can know there's a universe of people outside and you're responsible to it." Fine words, but their validity is undercut by our knowledge that Chris no more lives in that world outside than his father does, and his father has, at least, always known where he has lived. Similarly, Chris' criticism of America—"This is the land of the great big dogs, you don't love a man here, you eat him. That's the principle; the only one we live by. . . . This is a zoo, a zoo!"—is compromised by his own inability to put the great principle he presumably learned in the war into practice and his own inability to love. However narrowly his values are circumscribed by the family circle, Joe does love, Joe does live by another and better principle, one he is even willing to die for. The gunshot with which Joe ends his life casts Chris' fine words into a silent void because we know that, behind them, Chris is incapable of the commitment and love his father's suicide represents. Not only is Chris incapable of fulfilling his responsibility to the universe of people out there, he is even incapable of assuming his responsibility for the few people in here, in the enclosed back yard: his last words in the play are "Mother, I didn't mean to—." But he did, and that, too, Chris will have to learn to live with. . . .

"Where the son stands," Miller says in "The Shadow of the Gods," "is where the world should begin," but this does not happen in *All My Sons* anymore than it does in the "adolescent" plays Miller criticizes. It is undeniably true that "the struggle for mastery—for the freedom of manhood . . . as opposed to the servility of childhood—is the struggle not only to overthrow authority but to reconstitute it anew," but by this token Chris has achieved neither mastery nor manhood by the play's end. It might be argued that it is only after the play ends that Chris is equipped to make the world begin, to reconstitute authority anew, that is, only after he learns that his brother killed himself and watches his father do the same thing. If so, that is a high price in human life—to Miller, perhaps because he is not Christian, the highest price imaginable—to rouse Chris Keller to action. And, judging from Chris' past record, one cannot be sure that these two deaths will have that effect. The deaths of his comrades presented him with that opportunity before the play began and he has done nothing to reconstitute authority in their name. If we are to take Chris' stated sentiments about the men who died so that he might live seriously, then he is in the position at the beginning of *All My Sons* that Miller sees the Jewish psychiatrist in at the end of *Incident at Vichy:* his is "the guilt of surviving his benefactors" and whether he is "a 'good' man for accepting his life in this way, or a 'bad' one, will depend on what he makes of his guilt, of his having survived." By that criterion, Chris Keller is a bad man when *All My Sons* begins and he is no better when the play ends.

A Social Drama Infused with Tragic Undercurrents

Santosh K. Bhatia

All My Sons fulfills the aims and ends of social drama, but it nevertheless marks an important stage in Arthur Miller's artistic evolution toward full-scale tragedy. Santosh K. Bhatia notes that Joe and Chris Keller embody many of the conventions of Greek and Shakespearean tragedy. For instance, Joe Keller's mistaken commitment to his family over the well-being of society at large constitutes his "tragic flaw," for which he pays the ultimate price. Correspondingly, Chris Keller's realization of the greed and corruption that characterize modern society and his anguish over what to do about patriarchal crimes bear an indirect relation to Shakespeare's tragic hero Hamlet.

Compared with Miller's later plays, *All My Sons* is not a very powerful tragedy. Since it is one of his earliest plays Miller is still struggling to find the form. He is evidently trying to discover the tragic form that should be compatible with the aims and ends of social drama. It is predominantly a play of social responsibility yet Miller is able to transform it into tragedy. He tries to do that by providing a central tragic conflict, powerful scenes of confrontation and symbolic details. Being one of his first plays, it does not have the sophisticated structure of Miller's later ones, but it has a place of its own and can be seen as an important milestone in the growth of his tragic art. In fact, in one of his interviews, Miller was asked:

> Do you ever wish you could rewrite your plays after they have been produced? I've seen *All My Sons* described as an apprentice work for you. If you had the chance would you rewrite it?

Miller gave a negative reply and said:

No, I wouldn't know what to do with it. I just wouldn't know—
that's the way it is. It's a chapter of your life and there it is.

The play serves as an important chapter in its author's life
and it records a significant landmark in the progress of his
dramatic career on Broadway, particularly after the failure
called *The Man Who Had All the Luck*. What is still more important is that it paves the way for *Death of a Salesman* and
anticipates in many ways the thematic concerns of Miller's
successive plays. The emphasis of the play, no doubt, falls on
social realism, but it has the potential of a great tragedy.

THE TRAGIC DIMENSION

Critics have frequently failed to see anything beyond a traditional social play in *All My Sons*. [Critic] M.W. Steinberg ob-
serves: "It is most simply and clearly in the tradition of the
social problem plays of Ibsen, Shaw and Galsworthy."[1] In his
essay, Steinberg tends to reduce the play simply to the level
of a social allegory by suggesting that the characters are
mere illustrations of the forces working in "a selfish, mate-
rialistic society which respects economic success as it
flaunts underlying moral law. Similarly, [critic] Allan Stam-
busky remarks: "From the overall tone of *All My Sons*, Miller
seems more concerned with advocating a thesis or some
moral lesson than he is with portraying significant actions of
characters in relation to one another which makes for truly
tragic drama." It is certainly a social play, but it is not a thesis play in the manner of some of Ibsen's early ones or like
some plays of the thirties in America. [Dramatist] Sidney
Kingsley's *Ten Million Ghosts* (1936), dealing with munition
makers, can be called its forerunner. But, unlike *Ten Million
Ghosts*, *All My Sons* is not a play about war. It is much less
an anti-war play. It is a play about social relationships and
about the myopic vision of a selfish businessman who failed
to recognize his social responsibility. It is not merely a tale
of crime and punishment though apparently it seems to be
just that, but a play about confrontation and commitment.
Miller rightly points out:

> . . . the crime in *All My Sons* is not one that is about to be com-
> mitted but one that has long since been committed. There is
> no question of its consequences being ameliorated by any-
> thing Chris Keller or his father can do; the damage has been

1. Norwegian playwright Henrik Ibsen (1828–1906); Irish playwright and social critic
George Bernard Shaw (1856–1950); English novelist and playwright John Galsworthy
(1867–1933)

done irreparably. *The stakes remaining are purely the con-science of Joe Keller and its awakening to the evil he has done.*

The last sentence is important. The play's tragic import is contained in that and can be traced from there. The situation is given. An irreparable damage has already been done. The hero cannot walk away from it. What remains is the awakening of his conscience to the horror of his deed. In this respect the play has some affinity with Shakespeare's *Macbeth*. Like Macbeth, Joe Keller, too, works his way to prosperity through unscrupulous and dishonest means. Although he lacks the sensitiveness of Macbeth and does not suffer like him the qualms of a guilty conscience, he does realize the full horror of his deed and cannot escape its tragic consequences. The evil outside Macbeth is in part represented by Lady Macbeth and in part by the witches. Macbeth himself has the seed of ambition which is played upon and nurtured by these external force. Similarly, in *All My Sons*, the private guilt of the individual is matched against the larger social evil. Social pressures from the outside world work upon Joe Keller and make him do what he does. Miller strikes a subtle balance between individual responsibility and social pressures. He actually believes that "a writer has got to show both these things in operation: both the enormous pressure of circumstances and the individual act of choice." In this whole process he "berates society for its stultification of the individual but he also scorns the man who is a threat to the society."

JOE KELLER'S TRAGIC FLAW

All My Sons is the tragedy of a man who cannot see beyond his own family. Joe Keller, in this sense, has a myopic vision. He cannot see that a larger world exists outside his small family world. In caring too much for the prosperity of his own family, he jeopardizes the safety and security of society at large. Paradoxically his myopic vision is a gift of the same society against which he errs because it is based on the ethics of success. He is a product of society, and also its enemy. His mind and psychology are shaped and distorted by the capitalistic economic system and the chief motivating force behind his shortsightedness is the success-code of the society which he thoughtlessly follows. The myth of success and its counterpart, the fear of failure, compel him to do what he does. He knows that a failure in society cannot survive, so, in order to survive in the world of competition, he takes recourse to dishonest means. The important thing from the view point of tragedy, is that he lives on to realize his error. In the end, he realizes that he acted wrongly and was not simply acted upon.

In comparison with Miller's later plays, *All My Sons* has a straightforward plot. It has "a method one might call linear or eventual in that one fact or incident creates the necessity for the next." The social aspect of the problem it deals with, has been more sharply defined than in other plays. The central event of the play is a businessman's evasion of responsibility during war time which leads to the deaths of twenty-one pilots. But the treatment of this social theme is not so naive as to disallow all considerations of the play as a tragedy. "Its socialness," in Miller's own words, "does not reside in its having dealt with the crime of selling defective materials to a nation at war." That, according to Miller, could have been the subject of a crime-thriller or a detective story. "It is that the crime is seen as having roots in a certain relationship of the individual to society," which when not recognized can mean a jungle existence. No man can be an island unto himself; and in this sense alienation can be socially meaningful.

JOE KELLER'S BETRAYAL OF THE "POLIS"

In one of his early radio plays called *Grandpa and the Statue*, Miller touches upon the same question in a rudimentary manner and demonstrates the same theme that man needs society. Grandpa Monaghan refuses to contribute money for the pedestal of the Statue of Liberty. The play shows how he comes to realize that his decision was wrong. He realizes that he must be an integral part of the society in which he lives. *All My Sons* deals with an identical theme in a more serious manner through the perspective of a tragedy. Joe also thinks that he can prosper while others perish. He betrays his neighbour, Steve Deever, in the same manner as Eddie [Carbone] betrays his wife's relatives in [Miller's] *A View from the Bridge* and thus violates the sanctity and harmony of social relationships. His betrayal is even more grave and heinous because he not only betrays his neighbour but also the nation at war. On the social level, it amounts to the betrayal of one's community, one's "Polis" in the Greek sense of the word. As in the Greek tragedy, man who betrays his "polis" cannot prosper. In terms of the Greek tragedy, which Miller always kept in mind, the individual was to be at one with his society: Joe's tragedy is that he is not "at one" with his society.

The central conflict in the play is between familial and social obligations. It has been rightly observed:

> The thematic image of *All My Sons* is a circle within a circle, the inner depicting the family unit and the outer representing society, and the movement of the drama is concentric with the two circles revolving in parallel orbits until they ultimately coalesce.

To put it differently, the family and the society are like two pulleys, one smaller than the other but both joined together by a common axle so that the movement of one has a corresponding reaction on the other. The play depicts that man cannot disown society for his family. Keller does that. He isolates himself from others and thinks that his family can prosper at the expense of society. He does not see beyond his sons and his own family. What he says about his dead son, Larry, is actually true of himself:

> To him the world had a forty-foot front. It ended at the building line.

INDIVIDUAL TRAGEDY ARISES OUT OF SOCIAL CONDITIONS

He has a fanatic allegiance to a dream which is family centred. The tragedy occurs when he holds blindly to this dream and fails to recognize his place in society or when he gives up that place for the sake of his family dream. His trouble "is not that he cannot tell right from wrong but that his cast of mind cannot admit that he, personally, has any viable connection with his world, his universe, or his society." He is neither malignant nor villainous but one-sided and myopic. He is genuinely unable to foresee the public consequences of a private act. In order to appreciate this flaw in his character, it is important to understand his background and his profession.

He is a stolid and unintellectual businessman. He is also "an uneducated man for whom there is still wonder in many commonly known things." When the play opens he is discovered with a newspaper in hand. When asked about the news he says, "I don't read the news part any more. It's interesting in the want ads." A few minutes later, he reads— "wanted—Old dictionaries. High prices paid," and says, "Now what's a man going to do with an old dictionary?" Chris enters after some time and wants to read the book section of the newspaper. The following conversation ensues:

KELLER: What is that, every week a new book comes out?

CHRIS: Lot of new books.

KELLER: All different?

CHRIS: All different.

Keller says, "I don't know, everybody's getting Goddam educated in this country. . . . It's a tragedy: You stand on the street today and spit, you are going to hit a college man." He does not understand the difference between "brooch" and "broach." All this helps us understand his character and the low cast of his mind. He is an unimaginative and unlettered man. His actions have to be judged in the light of this background. Just as our knowledge of Willy Loman as a Salesman and of Eddie Carbone as a Longshoreman[2] helps us understand their psychology, our knowledge of Joe as an uneducated and unscrupulous businessman helps us judge his true character. His myopic vision is the product of his unenlightened mind in just the same way as Hamlet's philosophical vision is the product of his analytical mind. Chris confronts him at the end of Act II and asks him one question repeatedly: "Dad, you did it?" Keller pleads ignorance and speaks in a cracking voice: "I never thought they'd install them. I swear to God. I thought they'd stop them before anybody took off." He acts without the knowledge of the public consequences of his action. He also acts under a kind of fear-psychosis generated by socioeconomic pressures. The fear of losing his business and thus becoming a failure spawns a crisis of character in him. In a crucial speech he tells this to his son:

> I'm in business, a man is in business; a hundred and twenty cracked, you're out of business; you got a process, the process don't work you're out of business; . . . they close you up, they tear up your contracts, what the hell's it to them? You lay forty years into a business and they knock you out in five minutes, what could I do, let them take forty years, let them take my life away?

. . . Joe Keller acts under terrible pressures of a success-oriented society. He is afraid of reporting the defect or hold-

---

2. Willy Loman is the main character in *Death of a Salesman* (1949), and Eddie Carbone the main character in *A View from the Bridge* (1955).

ing the supply of airplane engines because that will ruin his business and consequently the future of his sons. . . . An excess of love for his sons makes Keller succumb to the socioeconomic pressures of society. The only motivation with him at the moment is to provide to his sons a future based on substantial wealth. He tells Chris: "What the hell did I work for? That's only for you, Chris, the whole shooting match is for you." Keller is called upon to play his role as a father on the one hand and as a citizen on the other, but his one-sidedness and disproportionate allegiance to his family make him ignore his role as a citizen. Miller explains this point:

> In *All My Sons* Joe Keller is a father and a citizen, but because he could not take the citizen side seriously he became less of a father and destroyed his own children. You literally have to survive with this whole because you can't survive without it.

In this respect *All My Sons* looks forward to [Miller's] *Incident at Vichy* (1964). The main idea in both the plays is that responsibility is not just a matter of personal relationships; it must also extend to the world at large. Joe's tragedy is that he does not understand this. He remains ignorant of the implications of his family centricity; not until the end of the play does he realize "the full loathsomeness of an anti-social action." Throughout the play he cannot think in terms of images other than filial or familial which is amply revealed in the following conversation between him and his wife:

> MOTHER: There's something bigger than the family to him (Chris).
>
> KELLER: Nothing is bigger!
>
> MOTHER: There is to him.
>
> KELLER: There's nothing he could do that I wouldn't forgive him. Because he is my son. Because I'm his father and he's my son. . . . Nothing is bigger than that. . . . I'm his father and he's my son, and if there's something bigger than that I'll put a bullet in my head!

When finally made to realize that there is something bigger than the family, that those who were killed (in Joe's own words) "were all my sons," he does put a bullet in his head.

Tragedy builds itself slowly in the play along the lines of this central conflict between the familial and the social. . . .

MYOPIA VERSUS EGALITARIANISM

The father and son conflict in the play is yet another variation of the same conflict between the familial and the social.

The family serves as a "symbolic cell" of the social structure. In the former version of the play, we are told, Miller had given the major role to Kate Keller and her astrological beliefs and the original title of the play was *The Sign of the Archer* but that did not succeed because the main conflict of the play did not emerge. "As the play progressed," says Miller, "the conflict between Joe and his son Chris pressed astrology to the wall." It is the backbone of the play. The confrontation between the father and the son actually springs from Chris's awareness of responsibility to others and his father's lack of it. We are prepared for this conflict from the beginning of the play, for Chris's character is the exact antithesis of his father's character. The antithetical nature of the two is made clear in the very beginning. He is an idealist whose entire allegiance is to society. He tells his father:

> I don't know why it is, but everytime I reach out for something
> I want, I have to pull back because other people will suffer.

Chris's concern for others has been polarized against his father's lack of concern for others. "The business," he says, "the business doesn't inspire me." He stands in direct contrast to his father. Dr. Jim Bayliss, their neighbour, says about Chris to his mother, "It takes a certain talent—for lying. You have it, and I do. But not him." Joe himself aptly sums up Chris's moral character in a moment of anger, when he says, ". . . everything bothers him. You make a deal, overcharge two cents, and his hair falls out. He don't understand money." Thus, Chris virtually serves as a foil to Joe. Set against Joe's myopic vision is Chris's egalitarian vision. He tells Ann that a realization dawned upon him when he was in command of a company during the war:

> It'd been raining several days and this kid came to me and
> gave me his last pair of dry socks. Put them in my pocket.
> That's only a little thing—but . . . that's the kind of guys I had.
> They didn't die; they killed themselves for each other. I mean
> that exactly; a little selfish and they'd've been here today. And
> I got an idea watching them go down. Everything was being
> destroyed, see, but it seemed to me that one new thing was
> made. A kind of responsibility. Man for man.

But afterwards when he comes home from the war, he finds it all different. He feels ashamed "to be alive, to open the bankbook, to drive the new car, to see the new refrigerator" because he feels it is "really loot and there's blood on it." The revelation of his father's guilt comes as a shock to him. He says:

> I know you're no worse than most men but I thought you
> were better. I never saw you as a man. I saw you as my fa-
> ther (Almost breaking): I can't look at you this way, I can't
> look at myself!

Through a number of speeches he lacerates his father. The
dominant feature of these speeches is the bestial imagery
which is deliberately used, it seems, to suggest that human
civilization is retreating into a jungle existence. The crisis
breaks upon Chris when he thinks in terms of society and
civilization. He says bitterly:

> This is the land of the great big dogs, you don't love a man
> here, you eat him! That's the principle; the only one we live
> by—it just happened to kill a few people that time, that's all.
> The world is that way, how can I take it out on him? What
> sense does that make? This is a zoo, a zoo!

This is certainly an appalling vision of society. The agony of
Chris is a dominating feature of the play. In his idealism he
reminds us of Prince Hamlet. He too, like Hamlet, confronts
a world which is full of evil and betrayal. In his speech, there
is the same note of questioning that we find in Hamlet's so-
liloquies. In fact, the interrogative note of his speeches
heightens the tragic import of the play because it touches
upon such questions of human behaviour, choice and responsibility that form the true subject of tragedy.

Joe Keller and Shakespeare's *Macbeth*

There may not be a depiction of prolonged suffering in the
play as it is in [Miller's] *Death of a Salesman* but there is an
overwhelming feeling of loss and grief. Keller's better self asserts itself strongly at the end and when it does, he becomes
tragic. His devotion to his sons is quite like that of Willy Loman who smashes his car only to make his sons rich. Joe is
also committed to the welfare of his children but the moment his humanity asserts itself over his selfish money in-
terests he shoots himself. There is the same single-minded
pursuit of an illusion in his case as in the case of Willy Loman. He too, has the same vehemence of a tragic hero and
holds firmly with an absolute commitment to the welfare of
his sons. Like Loman again, there is the same compulsive
drive towards death. The moment he discovers the gross-
ness and magnitude of his crime he takes a plunge and dies.

The most interesting feature of the play is how an anti-
social character is treated as a tragic hero. This is done by

focusing on his human aspect as against his commercial side so that we do not completely lose sympathy for him. All the time we are made aware that even his anti-social activities have behind them the human motivation of a father's love for his sons. As our sympathies are not completely lost for Macbeth even though he becomes a murderer, our sympathies for Joe are never alienated. It is the essential humanity in both which keeps them from becoming villains in our eyes and it is ultimately the assertion of their humanity against their debasement that makes them tragic.

CHAPTER 5

Contrasting Views

READINGS ON
ALL MY SONS

An Overly Contrived Play

Edward Murray

Arthur Miller spent two years writing *All My Sons*, and he revised it many times. He was rewarded for his commitment to *All My Sons* when the play became his first great critical and financial success; however, many critics have noted serious shortcomings in the play. Edward Murray offers an extended discussion of the major objections to *All My Sons:* the rather awkward plot contrivances, such as the appearance of Larry's letter; the perceived lack of depth and individuality in the characters; and a number of rather monotonous scenes that do not contribute to the play's dramatic development. Murray concludes by asserting that the play becomes bogged down in working its "thesis" (that there is "something bigger" than the family) too hard and that its tone is too preachy. Murray is a professor of English at the State University of New York, Brockport. Besides a book-length study of Arthur Miller, he has also written *Clifford Odets: The Thirties and After* and *Fellini the Artist.*

Although the structure of *All My Sons* is tight, it remains open to a number of serious criticisms. . . . Arthur Miller would have it that every step in *All My Sons* was carefully calculated. We need not necessarily accept this view. . . . Granting, for the sake of argument, that every move in the play was carefully plotted, one might question whether contrast, which is indeed a powerful dramatic device, could not have been established in a more economical manner, whether a relatively static and lengthy introduction threatening "boredom" was absolutely essential. A more cautious approach might suggest that Miller, in his second full-length play, had not as yet thoroughly mastered certain difficult problems of craft—chiefly, as Miller himself acknowledges, "the biggest single dramatic problem, namely, how to dramatize what has gone before."

A SLIP OF THE TONGUE REVEALS ALL

In addition, Miller seems guilty of having made his dramatic problem easy for himself at the turning point of the play. A "slip of the tongue" is certainly possible, but in the context of the play, is it not made to seem fortuitous? And is it not precisely the fortuitous nature of events that the form of the play is at pains to deny? According to Miller: "the structure of the play is designed to bring a man into the direct path of the consequences he has wrought"; and: "The fortress which *All My Sons* lays siege to is the fortress of unrelatedness." How is Kate's "slip of the tongue" related to the events of the play? Not only by intention, but through the achieved tightness of structure, Miller forces the reader to question the logic of his play. . . . In fact, there is no explanation given for Kate's "slip"—it must simply be attributed to chance. In dramatic terms, then, the "slip" is not made plausible. When one considers the events that immediately follow upon Kate's blunder, one is inclined to feel that Miller has not faced the dramatic task in a forthright manner.

MILLER USES ARBITRARY RESOLUTIONS

The arbitrary nature of the action continues in Act Three. Aside from the crude foreshadowing device . . . , Joe Keller shows no evidence of being a potential suicide. As a description of his character will reveal shortly, Joe is lacking in inner conflict; but if modern psychology has taught us anything, it is that none of us—least of all a suicide—is lacking in inner conflict. Kate, it should be noted, is made to threaten suicide in Act One; she says: "if [Larry's] not coming back, then I'll kill myself!" This, like Joe's threat in Act Three, looks like foreshadowing. It is beside the point to say that it is in character for Kate to choose life over death. Perhaps, one might argue, Miller intends that Kate's refusal to kill herself reflects freedom in the world of his play; it demonstrates that Joe is not being jerked about arbitrarily by the author, that Joe wills his own destruction. Whatever the rationale behind the strategy, however, it seems to make for confusion rather than complexity, for it tends to weaken Joe's motivation instead of making it appear freely chosen. The question arises:

Why *must* Joe kill himself? (One critic has speculated why Joe is strong enough to bear the guilt of his first act but not strong enough to shoulder the second guilt.) One is forced to conclude that Joe Keller kills himself because his suicide is an effective way to drive home the thesis.

The appearance of the letter in Act Three is the most censured device in the play. Only [critic] Dennis Welland defends it; he argues that the device is credible, economical, and dramatic. This is a valiant critical defense, but no more convincing, finally, than the play itself. As Kate brought about the turning point, Larry—a character never seen on stage—prepares the climax. The focus, it seems, should be on Joe, not Kate, or Larry, or even Chris. The audience should be made to see—should have been made to see from the first—the slow stages of Joe's movement toward self-destruction. This is why the leisurely introduction is blameworthy. Twenty-four hours is a short time in which to propel a man from "placidity" to a "rage of conscience." The letter itself might very well be "credible" and "economical"; this, however, is not enough. It is, for one thing, a stock device suggesting the "well-made play." Most critics, including the present one, are inclined to feel that the letter is not dramatically convincing. Contrivance also suggests itself in the stagy juxtaposition of Chris's indictment of his parents and the resounding report that immediately follows signalizing the end of Joe Keller's existence. This too is an "economical" and "dramatic" way to drive home the thesis.

WHO IS THE PLAY'S MAIN CHARACTER?

The question has been raised about who the protagonist is, structurally, in *All My Sons*. According to one critic, Miller never focuses clearly on Joe Keller; although Joe is central thematically, Chris appears to receive equal attention. According to a second critic, the interest shifts from the protagonist to the antagonist. . . . Until the final moments of the last act, Joe is relatively passive. Chris, however, forces the conflict from beginning to end. It is Chris who invites Ann to visit the Keller house; Chris who wants to remove the fiction of Larry's return; Chris who challenges Kate's obsession; Chris who calls Joe to defend his acts; Chris who demands that Joe atone for his crime against humanity. Although Joe carries the burden of the theme, then, Chris is the driving force within the structure. This dichotomy, I believe, damages the play. Not all plays, of course, have an active protagonist (which seems like a contradiction in terms); [Shakespeare's] *Othello* springs quickly to mind. One hesitates to generalize here, for each play must be viewed on its own merits. In *All My Sons*, the shift in emphasis would seem unhappy because Joe's movement toward suicide should be made credible, and, if that movement is to be made credible, the focus should be almost wholly on Joe. It is not that some dramatic "law" demands that Joe seal his own fate. It is that by the logic of *this* play, *All My Sons*, that Joe Keller must convincingly advance to his final gesture as a dramatic character.

LOOSE ENDS AND CONTRIVANCES

This raises, finally, several minor questions of probability. One critic has questioned the appearance of George in Act Two. George had not visited his father since the latter was sentenced to jail. Over three years had passed without George sending his father a Christmas card. Why, then, did George suddenly visit his father? George tells Ann: "I wanted to . . . tell him you were going to be married. It seemed impossible not to tell him." One might also consider the engagement of Chris and Ann. When Joe asks "why it has to be Annie," Chris says: "Because it is." Joe, baffled, points out that it is "five years" since Chris has seen Ann, but Chris says:

> I can't help it. I know her best. I was brought up next door to her. These years when I think of someone for my wife, I think of Annie. What do you want, a diagram?

Ann admits that she almost "got married two years ago," but that Chris started writing to her then and she had "felt something"—in fact, she had "felt something" ever since. She did not write, however, because: "I was waiting for you, Chris. Till then you never wrote. And when you did, what did you say? You sure can be ambiguous, you know." The reader suspects that Chris's "ambiguity" stems from his author's desire to save Ann for a crucial moment in the lives of his other characters. There is, in short, too much contrivance here. Why, after ignoring his father for three years, did George suddenly find it "impossible" not to inform the man of Ann's approaching marriage? Why this sudden necessity for respect? One might feel that there is no adequate reason here—except that Miller simply wanted George for the second act. Similarly, the romance between Chris and Ann does not encourage close scrutiny. There is something vague, even a little "mystical," about the coming together of the two lovers that suggests love less than manipulation. These are minor matters, however, and need not be overemphasized—they merely underline more important structural defects.

Ironically Miller, who had intended to write a play that would be "as untheatrical as possible," that would be distinguished by its "artlessness," actually produced the apotheosis of the theatrical and the artful—in other words, a "well-made play." And as [critic] William Archer says: "The trouble with the well-made play is that it is almost always . . . ill-made."

Are the characters in *All My Sons* "ill-made," too? . . .

THE PLAY FAILS IN ADEQUATELY REPRESENTING ITS CHARACTERS

Physically, none of Miller's characters is individualized in a striking way. Perhaps this is not a serious failing, however, in a form where there are actors to impersonate the playwright's creations. Certainly the stage directions characterize Joe sharply enough, and, as pointed out earlier, Miller reveals in action (to the point of "boredom"?) the features of Joe described in the directions. Although certain facts are related about Joe's background and social attitudes through dialogue, much else is also left blank. We learn nothing about Joe's parents, nothing about his childhood thoughts and feelings (a time, according to moralists and psychologists, when one's character is more or less molded for life), nothing about where Joe came from, nothing, save "the outskirts of an American town," about where he is at present. For a "realistic" play, the dialogue, then, is not wholly satisfactory. Psychologically, Joe has a number of traits; he is not presented under a single aspect. Nevertheless, he remains unsuitable for his specific role. More than an accumulation of traits are required here—the need is for contradictory traits that will directly influence the course of action. Joe Keller lacks these traits.

Dialogue similarly fails to reveal much, if anything, about Chris's childhood, boyhood, or young manhood. We learn only that Ann's family were neighbors to the Kellers while the children were growing. Chris, however, remains a more complex character than Joe. Chris, for example, is in conflict between the "love ethic" and the "business ethic," but Joe, presumably, feels no such conflict. Chris is also torn between loyalty to Ann and loyalty to his mother; between suspicion of Joe and the need to conceal his doubts from himself. If Joe is easier to believe in than his idealistic son, it is because Joe's philosophy seems to rise up palpably from the concrete and visible action on stage; but Chris must reach back to the past for an actualization of his philosophy (as Miller must reach back into the past for an unseen character to untie the knot). What we get is a *summary* of Chris's development rather than a *dramatic experience* of the thing itself. Consequently, Chris's "ideals" risk sounding too abstract—particularly when Chris, like Joe, yearns for family life and fortune, too. The fact that dialogue fails to illuminate Chris's background likewise militates against our belief in his values. Perhaps Miller is counting on a stock response here. Why should Chris differ from Joe and Kate? What specific factors account for the difference? The war experience does not seem entirely satisfactory as an explanation. Not all the fighting men were so "responsible"; not all the civilians regarded the war as a "bus accident." There is a danger of sentimentality here, the tendency to dichotomize humanity into "good guys" and "bad guys"— in short, a melodramatic vision. Lacking social depth, then, Chris often seems to step out of character to deliver a speech. Like other aspects of the play, the language is frequently too "neat," too obviously didactic.

At first sight, Kate Keller seems complex. A closer view, however, suggests that there is perhaps confusion interlaced with complexity in her characterization. It is Miller's attitude, as reflected in his stage directions, that are disconcerting. Miller says Kate has "uncontrolled inspirations"— but after threatening to kill herself, Kate manages to control her "inspiration." Miller says that Kate has an "overwhelming capacity for love"—but the play shows that her love has strict limits; like Joe's love, it has a "forty-foot front." Miller says that Kate feels pity for George—but the play shows that Kate, as much as Joe, destroyed George's family. This is not a problem in the theater; for an audience, Kate is a self-deceived woman; but for a reader, there is something incongruous in Miller's conception of Kate. Not satisfactory for either audience or reader, however, is the fact that Kate's dialogue fails to reveal anything at all about her background or development.

Only Chris really grows in the play. Joe is made to grow— and his "jump" is unconvincing. Kate is static. She has experienced some unpleasant events, but there is no indication that she has altered any of her basic attitudes. In Act One,

Chris feels guilty and vaguely suspects Joe; in Act Two, he learns the truth about Joe, but cannot immediately demand Joe's expiation—hence, his sense of guilt *increases*; but in Act Three, Larry's suicide reveals the course that Chris must take, and when the play ends, Chris is presumably free from his sense of guilt and able to enjoy life again. Although the letter device tends to weaken Chris's development too, his movement as a whole seems relatively steady and credible. There has also been preparation for his final action.

THE LIMITED ROLE OF THE MINOR CHARACTERS

None of the minor characters requires detailed discussion. All of them are "flat"; all of them are static. A few of them, such as Bert, Lydia, and Frank, seem superfluous in terms of action. Whether all of them are necessary to the development of the theme will be taken up below. Contrast is not very diverse here; Joe, Kate, Sue, and, to a lesser degree, Frank, are played off against Chris, Ann, George, and Jim. The contrast is a simple one—between those who have "ideals" and those who have no "ideals," or, at least, very limited ones. The minor characters are stock figures: Jim is the "country doctor"; Sue is the "shrew"; George is the "avenger." Frank, unlike the other minor figures, has an interesting psychology, but if you hold that a play should have no spare parts, a case could be made for Frank being unnecessary. Lydia and Bert have no discernible substance. Ann, of course, is the most disappointing character among the minor roles simply because of her position in the plot. A close reading of the text will yield next to nothing about Ann's background, traits, or social attitude. But perhaps these characters can be discussed with more profit in relation to the theme of the play. . . .

None of the minor characters seems absolutely essential to the theme. Frank, for example, appears unnecessary because whatever he might contribute to the meaning of the play is already inherent in Kate's role—one stargazer would seem sufficient. It might also be noted that the use of the stars is a crude way to focus the theme; it too overtly suggests "fate in the stars." Equally unfortunate is the too obvious play on Chris as "Christ." Only Ann and George are really integrated with the action. The others are there, no doubt, because Miller felt that their presence added complexity and social extension to the play. They add, in fact, no complexity. Structurally, they delay the point of attack, and that delay has repercussions on the credibility of Joe's development. Thematically, it is questionable whether they succeed in making the play more "significant." Where would one draw the line here? Is the formula: the more characters, the more extension and significance? It would not seem to be a mere matter of numbers. Economy demands that no character is strictly necessary who does not contribute something vital to action or theme. A more liberal view would leave room for a certain amount of "excess baggage" here—but Miller, it seems, has been rather too liberal on this score. In *Ghosts* (a play that many consider [Norwegian playwright Henrik] Ibsen's masterpiece), there are only five characters—half the number of *All My Sons*—yet Ibsen manages to project a complex social vision.

It has been asserted that *All My Sons* is actually a vote for the family instead of loyalty to the state ("something bigger" than the "family"), for, so the argument goes, Miller does not make clear whether the soldiers under Chris were devoted to an abstract ideal or merely attached to the group—if the latter, it is simply the family in disguise. Although Miller tends to idealize the American soldier, the abstract ideal in the play *is* precisely loyalty to one another, which might be described as a "family" loyalty, but obviously the "family" here extends beyond the narrow limits of one's immediate blood ties. It is an incomplete "family" loyalty only in the sense that it does not include the enemy.

I have suggested that *All My Sons* is a thesis play. Miller says: "I think now that the straight-forwardness of the . . . form was in some part due to the relatively sharp definition of the social aspects of the problem it dealt with." That the play is more complex than most critics, perhaps even including Miller, have allowed is certainly true. Whether it is complex enough, however, to weather the charge of thesis drama is another matter. Although Joe Keller and the other characters are not depicted as merely pawns of social forces, they *are* pawns of theatrical contrivance, a point which has been sufficiently discussed above. As for the "idea" itself, it would appear to be too explicitly insisted upon, too sermonic in deliverance, and, because sermons tend to oversimplify experience (even the laudable Sermon on the Mount has required volumes of exegesis), Miller seems guilty of ignoring the complexity of experience and the intractability of the human animal.

A Triumph of Concentrated Intensity

Dennis Welland

Upon its release in 1947, *All My Sons* indicated not only a substantial advance in the young Arthur Miller's playwriting skills, but also a triumph of realistic drama. For Dennis Welland, the enduring strength of the play lies in the fact that Miller manages to slowly strip away the surface contentment of the Keller family's life and expose the tensions and anxieties that lie beneath. By the end of *All My Sons*, the certainties on which the Kellers have based their lives have been shattered, and Miller forces his audience to confront the difficulty of maintaining one's moral focus in a world that is often highly immoral. Welland is a professor of American literature at the University of Manchester, England. He has written extensively on Mark Twain and Wilfred Owen, and founded the influential *Journal of American Studies*.

Both [*The Man Who Had All the Luck* and *All My Sons*] originated in real-life anecdotes that Henry Miller had heard, both have a mid-western setting and atmosphere, both are cast in the same dramatic mould. The fussily realistic detail of the set recurs in *All My Sons* but this time it is concentrated into one location throughout and an element of symbolism is introduced by the use of the tree. The cast-list is smaller than its predecessor by only one, and although the characters are, on the whole, more skillfully utilised, more fully developed, and more dramatically relevant, it is arguable that the sense of a neighbourhood community could have been more economically evoked. The small boy Bert is readily dispensable, and the Lubeys contribute little to the essential action.

Nevertheless, the advance on *The Man Who Had All the Luck* is evident both in theme and technique. An aircraft-engine manufacturer with no conscience who supplies faulty cylinder-heads in wartime is likely to command more attention and to raise wider issues than a mink-farming mechanic with a conscience at once too sensitive and too narrow. However, it is primarily at the domestic level that the problem is explored; the real value of the war framework lies in its topicality, in the audience-indignation that is universally generated against Joe Keller, and in the social tension and guilt set up in his sons. But there is never any question of these emotions prompting Chris to any form of political action or public protest—a point too obvious to need making, except that references to the play too often suggest that it is politically directed.

A TRIUMPH OF REALISM

Miller's achievement here, to put it at its lowest, lies in the verisimilitude with which he creates not only a convincing homely family, but also the sense of the flow of communal life in a suburban neighbourhood. The Kellers are part of a town in a way that the Beeves[1] never were. Indeed, the atmosphere of American neighbourliness is allowed to become so predominant that we are not kept sufficiently aware of the latent hostility to Joe that is mentioned from time to time.

Joe himself is too pleasant for the part he has to play. His betrayal of his partner seems out of key with his simple geniality and warmth of nature. As with most of Miller's characters, there is no vice in him, only littleness and his own form of myopia. He is genuinely unable to visualise the public consequences of what was for him a private act. To have stopped production when the flaw was discovered would have endangered the future of the business that meant security for his family: it was as simple as that. Keller is no villainous capitalist egged on by competitive mania in a cut-throat world of business, nor is he the cynical profiteer deliberately reducing the margin of safety in order to increase the margin of profit. Miller sees him as the simple man who has got on by energy and will power but who is hardly clever enough to know how he has done it. To this

---

1. The Beeves family appears in Miller's 1944 play *The Man Who Had All the Luck*.

extent he is another man who has had 'all the luck' and there is more than a grain of truth in his wife's comment to their son: 'We're dumb, Chris. Dad and I are stupid people. We don't know anything. You've got to protect us.' He is the ordinary man, surprised that 'every week a new book comes out', occasionally uncertain of his pronunciation, aggressively proud of his night-school education, yet moved to embarrassed facetiousness by his son's knowledge of French, and perplexed by a world where 'you stand on the street today and spit, you're gonna hit a college man.' Yet even these traits are only sporadically evident: it is the man's *bonhomie*, sense of fun, and good nature that predominate. If we come to accept the idea of this man deliberately allowing his partner to take the blame for shipping the faulty engines and thinking to patch up his conscience as easily as the flaws were patched to delay detection—and we do accept it in the theatre—it is primarily because of the dramatic effectiveness with which the climax and *dénouement* are brought about. Only later do we realise that it is in character, that it is the reverse of the coin of which the obverse has seemed so attractive, and that the coin is of smaller denomination than we thought, but none the less still a recognisable part of the currency.

MILLER USES TENSION TO GREAT EFFECT

The improvement in dramatic effectiveness may be immediately illustrated from the act-endings. In *The Man Who Had All the Luck* the direction 'Slow Curtain' repeated at the end of most of its five scenes recalls too readily Miller the student-dramatist who had had to ask a friend how long an act ought to be. There is not the climactic use of the curtain that is achieved naturally in *All My Sons* even in the first, relatively slow-moving act. The second act is brought to an explosive but perfectly-timed conclusion, and the superbly-developed tension of the play's ending is blurred only by the bringing of Chris back on to the stage for his mother's final and uncharacteristically wise comment. The impulse to prolong the action of *Death of a Salesman* beyond the death of its protagonist is more defensible than this, if only because the central issue of *All My Sons* is simpler and the suicide of Joe Keller dramatically more self-justifying, for the events leading up to it have been presented with a directness and an increasing tempo that make any alternative impossible. By contrast to Miller's skillful observance of the old unities in *All My Sons* the episodic structure of *The Man Who Had All the Luck*, with its dramatic confusion, loss of pace, and irrelevancies of character and action, seems almost amateurish.

The objection is sometimes made that *All My Sons* is so well-constructed as to be unconvincing, and the delayed revelation of Ann's third-act production of the letter from Larry is instanced as meretricious playmanship. On the other hand, her reluctance to produce it earlier is credibly enough explained by her, and it would not be easy to devise a more economical—or a more telling—method of bringing home the two things essential to the action at that point: the demolition of the mother's dream that her son is still alive and the demonstration to Joe, in terms that he cannot escape, of the consequences of his own conduct. Whether Ann, with that knowledge, would have been quite so sympathetic to Joe earlier in the play is another question, but one that Joe's irresistible geniality and Ann's nostalgia for the past go part of the way to answering, especially as she has earlier accepted the court's verdict that the blame was her own father's rather than Joe's.

THE PLAY PROGRESSIVELY UNDERMINES CERTAINTY

The confident certainty of dramatic movement here seems deliberately and successfully counterpoised against the loss of certainty that is the play's main theme. The keynote of the play is its questioning. Dialogue in the theatre is regularly carried on in terms of questions and answers, but in *All My Sons* the questions are in effect dialogue-stoppers. The dramatic power resides in the sort of questions asked and in the inability of the characters to answer them. Particularly prominent in the last act and in the exchanges between Joe and his son, this is observable throughout, and is responsible for the powerful climax to the second act in Chris's agonised reiteration of such questions as 'Where do you live, where have you come from? . . . What must I do, Jesus God, what must I do?' Nothing brings out Joe Keller's bewildered isolation better than this exchange with his wife:

KELLER: Maybe I ought to talk to [Ann]?

MOTHER: Don't ask me, Joe.

KELLER (*almost an outburst*): Then who do I ask? But I don't think she'll do anything about it.

> MOTHER: You're askin' me again.
>
> KELLER: I'm askin' you. What am I, a stranger? I thought I had a family here. What happened to my family?
>
> MOTHER: You've got a family. I'm simply telling you that I have no strength to think any more . . .
>
> KELLER: Then what do I do? Tell me, talk to me, what do I do?

A few minutes later, among questions to his son, he interjects the same plea: 'Talk to me'.

This is the bewilderment of a naturally garrulous man who has suddenly realised the impossibility of communication on the matters of deepest consequence, and it is a dilemma which the often-criticised banality of Miller's dramatic idiom is particularly well suited to suggest. Against these baffled questions and the clichés of his quotidian conversation Joe's final statement in the play stands out with an integrity and a force far in excess of its verbal content. His decision is made and his question answered by the letter of his dead son:

> MOTHER: You're so foolish. Larry was your son too, wasn't he? You know he'd never tell you to do this.
>
> KELLER: (*looking at letter in his hand*): Then what is this if it isn't telling me? Sure, he was my son. But I think to him they were all my sons. And I guess they were, I guess they were.

That is almost the only statement in this play of questioning that should be taken at its face value, and its quiet dignity makes Chris's summing-up ('there's a universe of people outside and you're responsible to it') superfluous and gratuitously didactic. The other and more sensational statements must be seen in their immediate context. 'This is the land of the great big dogs, you don't love a man here, you eat him! That's the principle'—it is not Miller who says this, but Chris, and Chris the baffled idealist *in extremis*. Its hysterical note distinguishes it from the more responsible tone of genuine recognition in Joe's speech. The play is a social drama, not as an attack on the capitalist business ethic, but as a study of the bewildered common man groping in a world where moral values have become a shifting quicksand, where you ask for guidance from others no surer than yourself, and when the simplest lesson—moral responsibility to others—is the hardest to learn.

Chronology

1915

Arthur Asher Miller is born in New York City on October 17, the second son of Isodore and Augusta Miller.

1921

Sister Joan is born.

1929

As a result of the depression, Isodore Miller's garment factory goes out of business, and the family is forced to move to Brooklyn to economize; Arthur takes on a variety of part-time jobs to support the family while going to high school.

1933

Arthur graduates from Abraham Lincoln High School but is refused admission to the University of Michigan because of poor grades; reapplies and is accepted in 1934.

1934

Studies journalism at the University of Michigan and playwriting with Professor Kenneth T. Rowe; contributes articles and eventually becomes an editor on the student newspaper, the *Michigan Daily;* becomes involved in many left-wing organizations on campus.

1936

Wins prestigious Avery Hopwood Award for his first play, *No Villain.*

1937

Wins his second Hopwood Award for *Honors at Dawn*; receives the Theatre Guild's Bureau of New Plays Award for *They Too Arise.*

1938

Receives runner-up Hopwood Award for *The Great Disobedience;* graduates and moves to New York.

1939

Writes scripts for Federal Theater Project until Congress cuts funding; writes radio plays for CBS and NBC.

1940

Marries Mary Grace Slattery.

1941–1943

Makes a living writing patriotic radio plays in support of the war effort.

1944

Tours army camps interviewing soldiers for his screenplay, *The Story of G.I. Joe;* Miller will later use these interviews as source material for his book *Situation Normal;* his first Broadway play, *The Man Who Had All the Luck,* closes after four performances; daughter Jane is born.

1945

Publishes *Focus,* a novel about anti-Semitism.

1947

All My Sons opens on Broadway, directed by Elia Kazan; it runs for 347 performances and wins the New York Drama Critics' Circle Award; son Robert is born.

1949

Death of a Salesman opens in New York, directed by Elia Kazan; it wins the Pulitzer Prize and the New York Drama Critics' Award.

1950

Miller adapts Henrik Ibsen's play *An Enemy of the People;* it closes after thirty-six performances, a failure Miller attributes to a growing right-wing, anti-intellectual climate in America.

1953

The Crucible opens in New York; reviewers debate its relevance to Senator Joseph McCarthy's "witch hunt" for former left-wing sympathizers in both the government and American society as a whole.

1954

The State Department denies Miller a passport to attend the opening of *The Crucible* in Brussels, claiming the denial is due to Miller's alleged support of the Communist movement and past left-wing activities; Miller claims it is because of *The Crucible*'s attack on Senator McCarthy's persecution of left-wing intellectuals in America; Miller meets Marilyn Monroe.

1955

A Memory of Two Mondays and the one-act version of *A View from the Bridge* are produced as a double bill in New York; Miller is attacked in newspapers for his leftist sympathies.

1956

The two-act version of *A View from the Bridge* opens in London; Miller testifies before the House Un-American Activities Committee, opening himself up to the possibility of criminal contempt charges for refusing to name individuals who attended meetings in the 1930s and '40s organized by Communist sympathizers; divorces Mary Slattery and marries Marilyn Monroe.

1957

Convicted and blacklisted for contempt of Congress; develops his short story "The Misfits" into a screenplay with Monroe in the lead role.

1958

Filming begins on *The Misfits;* U.S. Court of Appeals reverses Miller's contempt of Congress conviction.

1961

The Misfits is released; Miller divorces Marilyn Monroe.

1962

Miller marries photographer Inge Morath.

1963

Daughter Rebecca is born.

1964

After the Fall and *Incident at Vichy* open in New York to mixed reviews; Miller travels to Germany to report on trials of Nazi war criminals.

1965

Miller is elected president of PEN (Poets, Essayists, and Novelists), an international organization of writers; travels to the Soviet Union.

1968

The Price opens on Broadway; Miller serves as a Connecticut delegate at the Democratic National Convention in Chicago; supports the anti–Vietnam War candidacy of Eugene McCarthy.

1969

With Inge Morath, publishes travel journal *In Russia*; refuses to allow his works to be published in Greece as a protest against the Greek government's oppression of writers.

1970

In response to *In Russia*, Miller's works are banned in the Soviet Union.

1971

Miller is elected to the American Academy of Arts and Letters; helps win the release of Brazilian playwright and director Augusto Boal from prison; his commitment to the human rights of artists and writers throughout the world will continue throughout the 1970s and '80s.

1972

A comedy, *The Creation of the World and Other Business*, opens in New York but closes after only twenty performances.

1973–1977

Revivals of *Death of a Salesman* are produced in Philadelphia and New York; a television version of *After the Fall* is produced in 1974; *In the Country*, a travel journal collaboration with Inge Morath, is published in 1977; Miller petitions the Czech government to halt arrests of dissident writers.

1978

Theater Essays of Arthur Miller is published; Miller visits China with Inge Morath; participates in march on Soviet Mission in New York, protesting arrests and imprisonment of Soviet writers.

1979

Publishes *Chinese Encounters*, another travel journal collaboration with Morath.

1980

The American Clock opens at the Spoleto Festival in Charleston, South Carolina, to critical praise; however, in New York it closes after only a few performances; Miller publicly protests Israel's expansion of Jewish settlements on the West Bank; joins with other American writers in expressing support for the Polish Solidarity movement.

1982

Two one-act plays, *Some Kind of Love Story* and *Elegy for a Lady*, open in New Haven, Connecticut.

1983

Directs *Death of a Salesman* in Beijing, China, using a Chinese cast; successful Broadway revival of *A View from the Bridge.*

1984

Publishes *Salesman in Beijing,* another collaboration with Inge Morath; *Death of a Salesman,* with Dustin Hoffman as Willy Loman, plays to great acclaim on Broadway.

1985

Successful Broadway revival of *The Price;* Miller travels to Turkey to protest government persecution of writers; Dustin Hoffman's version of *Death of a Salesman* is produced on television.

1986

Revivals of *The Crucible* in New York and *All My Sons* in Connecticut; *Clara* is published.

1987

Autobiography *Timebends: A Life* is published as well as *Danger: Memory!* consisting of two one-act plays, *I Can't Remember Anything* and *Clara.*

1991

The Ride Down Mount Morgan opens in London.

1993

The Last Yankee opens in New York.

1994

Broken Glass opens in New York and London.

1995

Miller's eightieth birthday is celebrated in England with a Gala Performance at the Royal National Theatre in London and a Gala Dinner at the Arthur Miller Centre at the University of East Anglia in Norwich, England.

1996

Film version of *The Crucible,* starring Daniel Day Lewis and Winona Ryder, is released.

1998

Mr. Peters' Connections premieres in New York.

FOR FURTHER RESEARCH

BIOGRAPHICAL AND HISTORICAL WORKS

Christopher Bigsby, *Modern American Drama, 1945–1990*. Cambridge, England: Cambridge University Press, 1992.

Paul S. Boyer and Stephen Nissenbaum, *Salem Possessed: The Social Origins of Witchcraft*. Cambridge, MA: Harvard University Press, 1974.

Jean Gould, *Modern American Playwrights*. New York: Dodd, Mead, 1966.

Robert A. Martin and Steven R. Centola, eds., *The Theater Essays of Arthur Miller*. New York: Viking Press, 1978.

Arthur Miller, *Timebends: A Life*. New York: Grove Press, 1987.

Matthew C. Roudane, ed., *Conversations with Arthur Miller*. Jackson: University of Mississippi Press, 1987.

Ellen Schrecker, *Many Are the Crimes: McCarthyism in America*. Boston: Little, Brown, 1998.

Emily Watts, *The Businessman in American Literature*. Athens: University of Georgia Press, 1982.

Howard Zinn, *A People's History of the United States: 1492–Present*. New York: HarperPerennial, 1995.

CRITICISM

Christopher Bigsby, ed., *The Cambridge Companion to Arthur Miller*. Cambridge, England: Cambridge University Press, 1997.

Harold Bloom, ed., *Arthur Miller's* All My Sons. New York: Chelsea House, 1988.

Robert W. Corrigan, ed., *Arthur Miller: A Collection of Critical Essays*. Englewood Cliffs, NJ: Prentice-Hall, 1967.

Alice Griffin, *Understanding Arthur Miller*. Columbia: University of South Carolina Press, 1996.

Robert A. Martin, ed., *Arthur Miller: New Perspectives*. Englewood Cliffs, NJ: Prentice-Hall, 1982.

Benjamin Nelson, *Arthur Miller: Portrait of a Playwright*. New York: McKay, 1970.

June Schleuter and James K. Flanagan, *Arthur Miller*. New York: Ungar, 1987.

WORKS BY ARTHUR MILLER

Situation Normal [reportage]. New York: Reynal, 1944.

Focus [novel]. New York: Reynal, 1945.

All My Sons. New York: Reynal, 1947.

Death of a Salesman. New York: Viking Press, 1949.

An Enemy of the People [adaptation of play by Henrik Ibsen]. New York: Viking Press, 1950.

The Crucible. New York: Viking Press, 1953.

A View from the Bridge and *A Memory of Two Mondays*. New York: Viking Press, 1955.

Collected Plays. New York: Viking Press, 1957.

The Misfits [novel]. New York: Viking Press, 1961.

Jane's Blanket [juvenile]. New York: Collier, 1963.

After the Fall. New York: Viking Press, 1964.

Incident at Vichy. New York: Viking Press, 1965.

I Don't Need You Anymore [short stories]. New York: Viking Press, 1967.

The Price. New York: Viking Press, 1968.

In Russia [nonfiction, with Inge Morath]. New York: Viking Press, 1969.

The Portable Arthur Miller. Ed. Harold Clurman. New York: Viking Press, 1971.

The Creation of the World and Other Business. New York: Viking Press, 1972.

The Archbishop's Ceiling. New York: Dramatists Play Service, 1976.

In the Country [nonfiction, with Inge Morath]. New York: Viking Press, 1977.

The Theater Essays of Arthur Miller. Ed. Robert A. Martin. New York: Viking Press, 1978.

Up from Paradise [musical version of *The Creation of the World and Other Business*]. New York: Viking Press, 1978.

Chinese Encounters [nonfiction, with Inge Morath]. New York: Farrar, Straus, 1979.

The American Clock. New York: Viking Press, 1980.

Collected Plays: Volume 2. New York: Viking Press, 1980.

Elegy for a Lady. New York: Dramatists Play Service, 1984.

Salesman in Beijing [nonfiction]. New York: Viking Press, 1984.

Some Kind of Love Story. New York: Dramatists Play Service, 1984.

Playing for Time. Woodstock, IL: Dramatic Publishing, 1985.

Danger: Memory! Two Plays: "I Can't Remember Anything" and "Clara." New York: Grove Press, 1987.

"The Misfits" and Other Stories. New York: Scribner, 1987.

Timebends: A Life [autobiography]. New York: Grove Press, 1987.

The Golden Years. New York: Dramatists Play Service, 1990.

The Last Yankee. New York: Dramatists Play Service, 1991.

The Ride Down Mt. Morgan. New York: Viking Penguin, 1992.

Broken Glass. New York: Viking Penguin, 1994.

Homely Girl, a Life, and Other Stories. New York: Viking Press, 1995.

Mr. Peters' Connections. New York: Viking Press, 1998.

INDEX